Pure Comfort

150 All-Time Feel-Good Favorites

A Word About Weight Watchers

Since 1963, Weight Watchers has grown from a handful of people to millions of enrollments annually. Today, Weight Watchers is recognized as the leading name in safe and sensible weight control. Weight Watchers members form diverse groups, from youths to senior citizens, attending meetings virtually around the globe. Weight-loss and weight-management results vary by individual, but we recommend that you attend Weight Watchers meetings to benefit from the supportive environment you'll find there and follow the comprehensive Weight Watchers program which includes food plans, an activity plan, and a thinking skills plan. For the Weight Watchers meeting nearest you, call **800-651-6000.** For information on bringing Weight Watchers to your workplace, call **800-8AT-WORK.** Also, visit us at our Web site, **WeightWatchers.com,** or look for *Weight Watchers Magazine* at your newsstand or in your meeting room.

MEATBALL AND BARLEY SOUP, PAGE 75

WEIGHT WATCHERS PUBLISHING GROUP

EDITORIAL DIRECTOR	**NANCY GAGLIARDI**
ART DIRECTOR	**ED MELNITSKY**
PRODUCTION MANAGER	**ALAN BIEDERMAN**
OFFICE MANAGER AND PUBLISHING ASSISTANT	**JENNY LABOY-BRACE**
FOOD EDITOR	**EILEEN RUNYAN**
EDITOR	**CAROL PRAGER**
NUTRITION CONSULTANT	**PATTY SANTELLI**
PHOTOGRAPHER	**ANN STRATTON**
FOOD STYLIST	**MICHAEL PEDERSON**
PROP STYLIST	**CATHY COOK**
COVER PHOTOGRAPHER	**ALAN RICHARDSON**
COVER PROP STYLIST	**BETTE BLAU**
DESIGN/PRODUCTION	**LYNDA D'AMICO**

About Our Recipes

We make every effort to ensure that you will have success with our recipes. For best results and for nutritional accuracy, please keep the following guidelines in mind:

● Recipes in this book have been developed for Weight Watchers members who are following either the **Flex Plan** or the **Core Plan**® on the **TurnAround**® program. All **Core Plan** recipes are marked with our **Core Plan** recipe icon ☑. We include *POINTS*® values so you can use any of the recipes if you are following the **Flex Plan** on the program. *POINTS* values are assigned based on calories, fat (grams), and fiber (grams) provided for a serving size.

● All recipes feature approximate nutritional information; our recipes are analyzed for Calories (Cal), Total Fat (Fat), Saturated Fat (Sat Fat), Trans Fat (Trans Fat), Cholesterol (Chol), Sodium (Sod), Carbohydrates (Carb), Dietary Fiber (Fib), Protein (Prot), and Calcium (Calc).

● Nutritional information for recipes that include meat, poultry, and fish are based on cooked skinless boneless portions (unless otherwise stated), with the fat trimmed.

● We recommend that you buy lean meat and poultry, then trim it of all visible fat before cooking. When poultry is cooked with the skin on, we suggest removing the skin before eating.

● We follow the USDA guidelines for cooking meats and poultry to safe temperatures to prevent foodborne illness, but for beef and lamb (steaks, roasts, and chops) be aware that cooking them to the recommended minimum of 145°F will give you a medium-cooked steak, roast, or chop.

● Before serving, divide foods—including any vegetables, sauce, or accompaniments—into portions of equal size according to the designated number of servings per recipe.

● Any substitutions made to the ingredients will alter the "Per serving" nutritional information and may affect the **Core Plan** recipe status or the *POINTS* value.

● It is implied that all fresh fruits, vegetables, and greens in recipes should be rinsed before using.

PORK TENDERLOIN WITH
SUMMER FRUIT, PAGE 128

Contents

Smart Starters and Snacks

Best-Ever Buffalo Wings

⊙⊙

Hands-On Prep **25 MIN**
Cook **20 MIN**
Serves **8**

1 Wash the wings and pat dry with paper towels; cut off the tips and discard. Halve the wings at the joint, making about 24 pieces.

2 Combine the vinegar, broth, oil, and pepper sauce in a large zip-close plastic bag; add the chicken. Squeeze out the air and seal the bag; turn to coat the chicken. Refrigerate, turning the bag occasionally, about 30 minutes. Drain any remaining marinade.

3 Spray the broiler rack with nonstick spray and preheat the broiler. To make the dip, combine the cheese, yogurt, and mayonnaise in a small bowl.

4 Place the chicken on the broiler rack. Broil 5 inches from the heat until golden and cooked through, about 10 minutes on each side. Serve with the dip and celery.

3 pounds chicken wings (about 12), skinned
3 tablespoons apple-cider vinegar
2 tablespoons reduced-sodium chicken broth
2 teaspoons canola oil
2 teaspoons hot pepper sauce
¼ cup crumbled blue cheese
¼ cup plain fat-free yogurt
1 tablespoon reduced-fat mayonnaise
16 celery stalks, trimmed

PER SERVING (about 3 wing halves, 1 tablespoon dip, and 2 celery stalks): 117 Cal, 6 g Fat, 2 g Sat Fat, 0 g Trans Fat, 35 mg Chol, 137 mg Sod, 2 g Carb, 1 g Fib, 14 g Prot, 57 mg Calc. *POINTS* value: *3.*

Plan Ahead These zesty wings can be baked in advance to have on hand for an impromptu get-together. Refrigerate in a zip-close plastic bag up to 2 days. Just reheat in a 350°F oven about 15 minutes.

Sun-Dried Tomato and Sausage Focaccia

〜

Hands-On Prep **25 MIN**
Cook **20 MIN**
Serves **12**

1 Combine the water and sugar in a 2-cup measuring cup; sprinkle in the yeast and let stand until foamy, about 5 minutes. Stir in 2 teaspoons of the oil. Combine the flour and 2 teaspoons of the salt in a large bowl. Make a well in the center. Add the yeast mixture and stir gradually until the dough starts to gather around the spoon. Turn out on a floured surface; knead until the dough forms a smooth ball, 8–9 minutes.

2 Spray a large bowl with nonstick spray; place the dough in the bowl and spray with nonstick spray. Cover the bowl with plastic wrap and let the dough rise in a warm spot until doubled in size, about 40 minutes.

3 Cook the sausage in a large nonstick skillet over medium-high heat until well browned, stirring with a spoon to break it up into large pieces. Let cool.

4 Preheat the oven to 450°F. Spray a 10½ x 15½-inch jelly-roll pan with nonstick spray. Punch down the dough. Spread one third of the sausage, the tomato, and rosemary over the top. Fold the dough in half over the mixture, then repeat twice to incorporate the mixture. Press the dough into the pan. Cover and let stand until puffed, 10 minutes. Bake until golden, 20–22 minutes. Brush with the remaining oil and sprinkle with the remaining salt. Cut into 12 pieces.

1⅔ cups warm water
   (105–115°F)
¼ teaspoon sugar
1 package quick-rise yeast
3 teaspoons olive oil
3¾ cups all-purpose flour
2¼ teaspoons kosher salt
1½ links (6 ounces) sweet
   Italian turkey sausage,
   casings removed
1 tablespoon minced
   drained oil-packed
   sun-dried tomatoes
1 tablespoon minced fresh
   rosemary or thyme

Per serving (1 piece): 183 Cal, 3 g Fat, 1 g Sat Fat, 0 g Trans Fat, 10 mg Chol, 455 mg Sod, 30 g Carb, 1 g Fib, 7 g Prot, 11 mg Calc.
POINTS value: *4.*

THE ULTIMATE CRAB COCKTAIL

The Ultimate Crab Cocktail

❧

Hands-On Prep **20 MIN**
Cook **NONE**
Serves **4**

1 Combine the chili sauce, horseradish, and 3 teaspoons of the lemon juice in a small bowl. Cover and refrigerate until ready to serve.

2 Combine the crabmeat, celery, red onion, the remaining 2 teaspoons of lemon juice, and the tarragon in a medium bowl; mix gently. Serve at once with the cocktail sauce or cover and refrigerate up to 8 hours and serve chilled.

½ **cup prepared chili sauce**
4 **teaspoons grated horseradish in vinegar, drained**
5 **teaspoons fresh lemon juice**
¾ **pound fresh cooked jumbo lump crabmeat, picked over**
1 **celery stalk, finely chopped**
⅓ **cup finely chopped red onion**
1 **tablespoon chopped fresh tarragon**

PER SERVING (½ cup crabmeat with 2 tablespoons sauce): 126 Cal, 2 g Fat, 0 g Sat Fat, 0 g Trans Fat, 85 mg Chol, 609 mg Sod, 10 g Carb, 1 g Fib, 18 g Prot, 105 mg Calc. **POINTS** value: **2.**

How We Did It To make the most stunning cocktail, we started with chunks of lump or jumbo lump crabmeat (as opposed to pasteurized canned or frozen crabmeat, which comes in smaller pieces). Look for jumbo lump crabmeat in fish markets or better supermarkets. Serve the cocktail plain or with crisp rounds of melba toast; 6 rounds with each serving will increase the **POINTS** value by **1.**

Nachos Deluxe

⬧⬥

Hands-On Prep **15 MIN**
Cook **15 MIN**
Serves **8**

1 Preheat the oven to 425°F. Spray a large baking sheet with nonstick spray and set aside.

2 Heat the oil in a large nonstick skillet over medium-high heat. Add the chicken and onion; cook, stirring with a wooden spoon to break up the chicken, until browned, about 3 minutes. Add the tomatoes, beans, Mexican seasoning, and salt; cook, stirring occasionally, until thickened, about 5 minutes. Remove the skillet from the heat and keep warm.

3 Spread the tortilla chips on the baking sheet. Sprinkle with the cheese, olives, and peppers. Bake just until the cheese melts, about 5 minutes. Transfer the nachos to a serving platter. Top with the chicken mixture and sour cream. Serve at once.

PER SERVING (1¼ cups): 204 Cal, 4 g Fat, 2 g Sat Fat, 0 g Trans Fat, 17 mg Chol, 483 mg Sod, 29 g Carb, 4 g Fib, 13 g Prot, 141 mg Calc. *POINTS* value: *4.*

Good Idea Vary the nacho topping to suit your mood. Try canned black or pinto beans or substitute reduced-fat cheddar for the Monterey Jack cheese.

1 teaspoon canola oil
¼ pound ground skinless chicken breast
1 small onion, chopped
1 (14½-ounce) can diced tomatoes with green chiles
1 cup rinsed and drained canned red kidney beans
2 teaspoons Mexican seasoning
¼ teaspoon salt
6 ounces reduced-fat restaurant-style tortilla chips
¾ cup shredded reduced-fat Monterey Jack cheese
12 pitted small black olives, sliced
¼ cup sliced pickled jalapeño peppers, drained
½ cup fat-free sour cream

Cajun Shrimp with Old Bay Mayonnaise

❧

Hands-On Prep **10 MIN**
Cook **3 MIN**
Serves **4**

☑

1 Combine the mayonnaise, scallion, garlic, lemon juice, and Old Bay seasoning in a small bowl.

2 Combine the shrimp and the Cajun seasoning in a medium bowl.

3 Heat the oil in a large nonstick skillet over medium-high heat. Add the shrimp and cook just until lightly browned and opaque in the center, 1½–2 minutes on each side. Serve at once with the Old Bay mayonnaise.

PER SERVING (6 shrimp with 3 tablespoons Old Bay mayonnaise): 142 Cal, 5 g Fat, 1 g Sat Fat, 0 g Trans Fat, 173 mg Chol, 737 mg Sod, 7 g Carb, 1 g Fib, 18 g Prot, 40 mg Calc. *POINTS* value: **3.**

¾ cup fat-free mayonnaise
1 scallion, finely chopped
1 garlic clove, minced
2 teaspoons fresh
   lemon juice
¾ teaspoon Old Bay
   seasoning
1 pound peeled and
   deveined large shrimp
1½ teaspoons Cajun
   seasoning
2 teaspoons olive oil

Food Note What's the difference between Old Bay seasoning and Cajun seasoning? Both are great with seafood and contain a good dose of cayenne, but Old Bay also has an assortment of "sweet" spices (allspice, ginger, mace, cardamom, and cinnamon) to balance the heat.

Classic Deviled Eggs

❧

Hands-On Prep **20 MIN**
Cook **25 MIN**
Serves **6**

1 Place the eggs in a saucepan large enough to hold them in a single layer; add enough cold water to cover. Bring to a boil over medium-high heat; reduce the heat and cook at a bare simmer 12 minutes. Rinse the eggs under cold water. When cool enough to handle, remove the shells.

2 To make the filling, halve the eggs lengthwise. Place the yolks of 4 eggs in a medium bowl and discard the remaining yolks. Chop the whites of 2 eggs and add to the bowl; mash well with a fork. Add the celery, carrot, scallion, sour cream, mayonnaise, mustard, vinegar, salt, and pepper; blend with a fork.

3 Spoon the filling into the hollows of the remaining 12 egg-white halves, mounding to fill. Place on a platter, cover with plastic wrap, and refrigerate until cold, at least 1 hour.

- 8 large eggs
- 1 small celery stalk, finely chopped (about ¼ cup)
- 1 small carrot, shredded (about ¼ cup)
- 2 tablespoons thinly sliced scallion
- 2 tablespoons fat-free sour cream
- 1 tablespoon low-fat mayonnaise
- 2 teaspoons Dijon mustard
- 1 teaspoon red-wine vinegar
- ¼ teaspoon salt
- ¼ teaspoon freshly ground pepper

PER SERVING (2 stuffed-egg halves): 73 Cal, 4 g Fat, 1 g Sat Fat, 0 g Trans Fat, 142 mg Chol, 232 mg Sod, 3 g Carb, 0 g Fib, 7 g Prot, 36 mg Calc. *POINTS* value: *2.*

Make It Core If you're following the **Core Plan**, just substitute fat-free mayonnaise for the low-fat variety.

Enlightened Swiss Fondue

❧

Hands-On Prep **20 MIN**
Cook **20 MIN**
Serves **10**

1 Put the beans and milk in a food processor and puree, scraping the sides of the bowl frequently, until completely smooth, about 3 minutes.

2 Rub a medium nonreactive saucepan with the garlic; discard the garlic. Pour the wine into the saucepan and bring to a simmer over medium heat. Add the Gruyère and Asiago cheeses, a handful at a time, stirring constantly with a wooden spoon in a zigzag motion, until the cheese is melted, 5–8 minutes (do not boil, or the cheese will form clumps).

3 Meanwhile, whisk together the water and cornstarch in a cup until smooth. Stir the bean mixture, dissolved cornstarch, kirsch, and nutmeg into the cheese mixture; cook, stirring gently, until smooth and slightly thickened, 5–6 minutes. Transfer to a large fondue pot and set over moderate heat. Serve at once with bread, vegetables, or apple.

PER SERVING (about ⅔ cup fondue with 1 ounce cubed bread, ½ cup broccoli florets, or ½ cup sliced apple): 141 Cal, 6 g Fat, 3 g Sat Fat, 0 g Trans Fat, 19 mg Chol, 171 mg Sod, 14 g Carb, 3 g Fib, 8 g Prot, 205 mg Calc. *POINTS* value: *3.*

1 (19-ounce) can **cannellini (white kidney) beans, rinsed and drained**
½ **cup reduced-fat (2%) milk**
½ **small garlic clove**
¾ **cup dry white wine**
5 **ounces Gruyère cheese, shredded (about 1¾ cups)**
1 **ounce coarsely shredded aged Asiago cheese (about ⅓ cup)**
1 **tablespoon water**
2 **teaspoons cornstarch**
1 **tablespoon kirsch**
⅛ **teaspoon ground nutmeg**
10 **ounces crusty French-bread cubes (5 cups)**
Steamed vegetables (such as broccoli and carrots), and/or slices of tart apple

Zap It Got leftover fondue? Transfer it to a large microwavable bowl, cover, and refrigerate up to 3 days. To reheat, cover loosely with wax paper and cook on 50 percent power, stirring every 10 seconds or so, just until melted.

Zesty Cheese Ball

❧

Hands-On Prep **15 MIN**
Cook **NONE**
Serves **16**

1 Put the cheddar cheese, cottage cheese, mustard, and cayenne in a food processor and pulse until very smooth, about 2 minutes. Add the cream cheese and soup mix; process until smooth, scraping down the sides of the bowl as needed. Scrape with a spatula onto a large sheet of plastic wrap.

2 Wrap the plastic around the cheese mixture and with your hands shape it into a 4-inch ball or a 7-inch log. Refrigerate until firm, at least 3 hours or overnight.

3 Just before serving, sprinkle about half the parsley in a circle on a sheet of plastic wrap. Unwrap the cheese ball or log and place it on the parsley. Sprinkle the remaining parsley on top of the ball or log and press to help it adhere. Carefully roll any uncoated areas in the loose parsley, and adjust the shape if necessary. Serve with the vegetables.

¾ cup shredded reduced-fat sharp cheddar cheese
¾ cup reduced-fat (2%) cottage cheese
1 tablespoon Dijon mustard
⅛ teaspoon cayenne
1 (8-ounce) package fat-free cream cheese, cut into quarters, at room temperature
1 (9-ounce) envelope dry vegetable-soup recipe mix
½ cup chopped fresh parsley
4 cups assorted vegetables, (such as carrots, celery, and bell peppers), cut-up

PER SERVING (2 tablespoons cheese mixture with ¼ cup vegetables): 45 Cal, 2 g Fat, 1 g Sat Fat, 0 Trans Fat, 6 mg Chol, 303 mg Sod, 3 g Carb, 0 g Fib, 5 g Prot, 78 mg Calc. ***POINTS*** value: *1.*

Food Note For a somewhat firmer texture, substitute an equal amount of pot cheese for the cottage cheese. In addition to cut-up veggies, scatter a few reduced-sodium saltines for guests to munch on; 4 crackers will increase the per-serving ***POINTS*** value by *1.*

Party Cheese Puffs

Hands-On Prep **30 MIN**
Cook **30 MIN**
Serves **15**

1 Bring the milk, butter, mustard powder, salt, and pepper to a boil in a medium saucepan; reduce the heat to medium. Beat in the flour and Asiago cheese with a wooden spoon, stirring vigorously, until the mixture leaves the sides of the pan. Remove the pan from the heat and let the mixture cool 10 minutes.

2 Meanwhile, adjust the racks to divide the oven into thirds; preheat the oven to 400°F. Line two baking sheets with foil and lightly coat with nonstick spray.

3 With an electric mixer on medium speed, beat the eggs into the flour mixture until well blended. Sift in the baking powder; then add the egg whites and continue beating until the mixture is glossy and smooth. Decrease the speed to low and beat in the cheddar cheese just until combined.

4 Spoon the dough into a pastry bag or a plastic food-storage bag with a corner cut off. Pipe the dough onto the baking sheets in 1-inch mounds, spacing the mounds 1 inch apart (you may pipe the dough into 1½-inch-long "fingers" if you prefer), making about 75 puffs (or fingers). Bake until golden brown and firm to the touch, about 22 minutes. Transfer to a rack and serve hot or warm.

1 (12-ounce) can
  evaporated fat-free milk
2 tablespoons unsalted
  butter
¾ teaspoon mustard powder
¾ teaspoon salt
¼ teaspoon freshly
  ground pepper
1 cup all-purpose flour
⅓ cup grated Asiago cheese
2 large eggs
1 teaspoon baking powder
3 egg whites
½ cup shredded reduced-fat
  cheddar cheese

PER SERVING (5 puffs): 96 Cal, 4 g Fat, 2 g Sat Fat, 0 g Trans Fat, 37 mg Chol, 255 mg Sod, 9 g Carb, 0 g Fib, 6 g Prot, 147 mg Calc. ***POINTS*** value: **2.**

Roasted Asparagus with Cucumber-Cilantro Dip

❧

Hands-On Prep **10 MIN**
Cook **5 MIN**
Serves **4**

☑

1 Preheat the oven to 425°F. Spray a large rimmed baking sheet with olive oil nonstick spray.

2 To make the dip, combine the yogurt, cucumber, cilantro, garlic, lime zest, and ¼ teaspoon of the salt in a small bowl.

3 Combine the asparagus, oil, the remaining ½ teaspoon of salt, and the pepper in a large bowl; toss to coat. Spread the asparagus in a single layer on the baking sheet. Bake, shaking the pan occasionally, until the asparagus are crisp-tender, 6–10 minutes (depending on their thickness). Let cool slightly, about 10 minutes. Serve warm, or at room temperature, with the dip.

1 (6-ounce) container plain fat-free yogurt
½ cucumber, peeled, seeded, and finely chopped
1 tablespoon chopped fresh cilantro
1 garlic clove, minced
1 teaspoon grated lime zest
¾ teaspoon salt
1 pound fresh asparagus, trimmed
2 teaspoons extra-virgin olive oil
⅛ teaspoon freshly ground pepper

PER SERVING (about 5 asparagus with 3 tablespoons dip): 58 Cal, 3 g Fat, 0 g Sat Fat, 0 g Trans Fat, 1 mg Chol, 468 mg Sod, 7 g Carb, 1 g Fib, 4 g Prot, 74 mg Calc. *POINTS* value: *1*.

Plan Ahead Preparing the dip in advance will allow the flavors to develop and save you time too. The dip will keep in an airtight container in the refrigerator up to 3 days.

Spiced Edamame

⌘

Hands-On Prep **5 MIN**
Cook **20 MIN**
Serves **6**

1 Cook the edamame according to the package directions; drain.

2 Heat the oil in a large nonstick skillet over medium-high heat. Add the edamame, salt, cumin, and pepper; cook, stirring frequently, until fragrant, about 1 minute. Serve at once.

PER SERVING (about ⅓ cup): 108 Cal, 4 g Fat, 0 g Sat Fat, 0 g Trans Fat, 0 mg Chol, 418 mg Sod, 9 g Carb, 4 g Fib, 8 g Prot, 52 mg Calc. **POINTS** value: **2.**

1 (16-ounce) package frozen unshelled edamame (green soybeans)
1 teaspoon olive oil
1 teaspoon salt
½ teaspoon ground cumin
¼ teaspoon freshly ground pepper

Food Note Cooking the edamame in their shells keeps them crisp-tender. Although the shells are not edible, you can easily extract the beans from their shells and still savor the delicious seasoning.

Cinnamon Apple-Pear Kebabs

Hands-On Prep **10 MIN**
Cook **10 MIN**
Serves **4**

1 Spray the broiler rack with canola oil nonstick spray and preheat the broiler.

2 Combine the pears, apples, brown sugar, and oil in a large bowl. Add the lemon juice and cinnamon; toss to coat. Alternately thread 3 pear chunks and 3 apple chunks on each of 8 (12-inch) metal or wooden skewers; place the skewers on the broiler rack. Broil 5 inches from the heat, turning every 2 minutes, until the fruit is crisp-tender and lightly browned, 7–8 minutes. Let the kebabs cool about 10 minutes; serve warm.

2 large Bartlett pears, peeled and cut into 12 chunks apiece
2 large Golden Delicious apples, peeled and cut into 12 chunks apiece
1 teaspoon packed brown sugar
1 teaspoon canola oil
1 tablespoon fresh lemon juice
½ teaspoon cinnamon

PER SERVING (2 kebabs): 88 Cal, 2 g Fat, 0 g Sat Fat, 0 g Trans Fat, 0 mg Chol, 4 mg Sod, 20 g Carb, 3 g Fib, 1 g Prot, 10 mg Calc. *POINTS* value: *1.*

Plan Ahead If using wooden skewers, soak them in water first for about 30 minutes. Because the lemon juice helps keep the fruit from turning brown, you can refrigerate the fully assembled kebabs, well wrapped in plastic wrap, up to 2 hours ahead.

CURRIED POPCORN; CINNAMON
APPLE-PEAR KEBABS, PAGE 23

Curried Popcorn

Hands-On Prep **5 MIN**
Cook **5 MIN**
Serves **8**

1 Heat the oil in a large pot over medium-high heat. Add the popcorn and cook, covered, shaking the pot occasionally, until hot, about 3 minutes.

2 Stir in the salt, curry powder, cumin, coriander, and cayenne; cook, covered, shaking the pot constantly, until the popcorn pops, 3–4 minutes.

PER SERVING (2 cups): 91 Cal, 3 g Fat, 0 g Sat Fat, 0 g Trans Fat, 0 mg Chol, 437 mg Sod, 14 g Carb, 3 g Fib, 2 g Prot, 6 mg Calc. **POINTS** value: *1.*

4 teaspoons extra-virgin olive oil
¾ cup unpopped popcorn
1½ teaspoons salt
1½ teaspoons curry powder
1 teaspoon ground cumin
¾ teaspoon ground coriander
⅛ teaspoon cayenne

Good Idea If you want to add a sweet note to this snack, stir 1 cup dried currants into the popped popcorn. Just remember to increase the **POINTS** value for each serving by *1.*

Great Breakfasts and Brunches

Bacon-and-Egg Muffin Melt

Hands-On Prep **5 MIN**
Cook **5 MIN**
Serves **1**

1 Toast the English muffin.

2 Meanwhile, spray a small nonstick skillet with nonstick spray and set over medium-high heat. Add the egg and cook until the white begins to set, about 1 minute. Break the yolk and cook about 30 seconds. Flip and cook until the yolk is set, about 1 minute.

3 Place half the muffin on a plate. Top with the egg and set aside.

4 Add the bacon to the skillet and cook until heated through, about 30 seconds. Turn and top with the cheese. Cook, covered, until the cheese melts, about 30 seconds. Place the bacon and cheese on top of the egg. Spread the ketchup over the cheese and top with the remaining muffin half. Serve at once.

PER SERVING: 270 Cal, 8 g Fat, 2 g Sat Fat, 0 g Trans Fat, 229 mg Chol, 839 mg Sod, 28 g Carb, 3 g Fib, 22 g Prot, 259 mg Calc.
POINTS value: **5.**

Good Idea Vary this quick and delicious breakfast sandwich by using deli-sliced ham or turkey instead of the Canadian bacon and fat-free Swiss or mozzarella instead of the cheddar cheese.

1 whole-wheat English muffin, split
1 large egg
1 slice Canadian bacon
1 (½-ounce) slice fat-free cheddar cheese
1 teaspoon ketchup

Fines Herbes Omelette

❧

Hands-On Prep **5 MIN**
Cook **3 MIN**
Serves **1**

✓

1 Beat the egg, egg whites, milk, parsley, chives, tarragon, salt, and pepper in a medium bowl.

2 Spray a small nonstick skillet with canola oil nonstick spray and set over medium-high heat. When a drop of water sizzles on the skillet, pour in the egg mixture and swirl to cover. Cook until the underside starts to set, about 20 seconds. Gently stir with a heatproof spatula and cook, stirring occasionally to allow the uncooked egg to run underneath, until the eggs are set but slightly runny on top, 1–2 minutes. Fold the omelette into thirds and cook just until set, about 30 seconds longer. Slide the omelette onto a plate and serve at once.

1 large egg
2 egg whites
1 tablespoon fat-free milk
2 teaspoons chopped
  fresh parsley
2 teaspoons chopped
  fresh chives
1 teaspoon chopped
  fresh tarragon
¼ teaspoon salt
⅛ teaspoon freshly
  ground pepper

PER SERVING: 116 Cal, 5 g Fat, 2 g Sat Fat, 0 g Trans Fat, 213 mg Chol, 764 mg Sod, 3 g Carb, 0 g Fib, 14 g Prot, 58 mg Calc. *POINTS* value: *3.*

Good Idea Top the omelette with 1 tablespoon shredded fat-free cheddar or Swiss cheese. The per-serving *POINTS* value will remain the same.

Scrambled Eggs with Ricotta, Tomatoes, and Basil

Hands-On Prep **10 MIN**
Cook **5 MIN**
Serves **2**

Heat the oil in a large nonstick skillet over medium-high heat. Add the onion and garlic; cook, stirring occasionally, until the onion softens, 1–2 minutes. Stir in the tomatoes and cook, stirring occasionally, until softened, 1–2 minutes. Add the cheese and cook, stirring occasionally, until heated, about 20 seconds. Add the egg substitute, basil, salt, and pepper; cook, stirring occasionally, just until the egg mixture is set, about 2 minutes. Serve at once.

PER SERVING (1 cup): 149 Cal, 3 g Fat, 0 g Sat Fat, 0 g Trans Fat, 7 mg Chol, 592 mg Sod, 13 g Carb, 2 g Fib, 17 g Prot, 128 mg Calc. *POINTS* value: *3.*

Food Note If you want to serve 4, simply double all the ingredients, but use three quarters of an onion and 3 garlic cloves.

1 teaspoon extra-virgin olive oil
½ onion, chopped
2 garlic cloves, minced
1 cup cherry tomatoes, halved
⅓ cup fat-free ricotta cheese
1 cup fat-free egg substitute
2 tablespoons chopped fresh basil
¼ teaspoon salt
⅛ teaspoon freshly ground pepper

SCRAMBLED EGGS WITH RICOTTA, TOMATOES, AND BASIL; ORANGE-CRANBERRY SCONES, PAGE 50

Eggs Pipérade

❧❧

Hands-On Prep **10 MIN**
Cook **10 MIN**
Serves **4**

☑

1 Whisk together the eggs, egg whites, ½ teaspoon of the salt, and ⅛ teaspoon of the ground pepper in a medium bowl; set aside.

2 Heat the oil in a large nonstick skillet over medium-high heat. Add the onion and garlic; cook, stirring occasionally, until the onion softens, 1–2 minutes. Add the bell peppers, basil, thyme, and the remaining ¼ teaspoon of salt and ⅛ teaspoon ground pepper; cook, stirring occasionally, until the vegetables are tender, 5–6 minutes. Add the tomatoes and cook, stirring occasionally, until softened, about 3 minutes. Stir in the egg mixture and cook, covered, until set, 3–4 minutes (but do not stir). Cut into 4 wedges.

PER SERVING (1 wedge): 122 Cal, 6 g Fat, 2 g Sat Fat, 0 g Trans Fat, 159 mg Chol, 531 mg Sod, 8 g Carb, 2 g Fib, 9 g Prot, 42 mg Calc. **POINTS** value: *3.*

Good Idea These French-style eggs are lovely served with a chunk of toasted baguette. A 1-ounce piece with each serving will increase the **POINTS** value by *2.* Just remember to deduct it from your **weekly POINTS Allowance.**

3 large eggs
3 egg whites
¾ teaspoon salt
¼ teaspoon freshly ground pepper
2 teaspoons extra-virgin olive oil
1 small onion, finely chopped
2 garlic cloves, minced
1 large red bell pepper, seeded and finely chopped
1 small green bell pepper, seeded and finely chopped
1 teaspoon dried basil
¼ teaspoon dried thyme
3 plum tomatoes, seeded and chopped

Asparagus and Roasted-Pepper Frittata

❧❧

Hands-On Prep **15 MIN**
Cook **15 MIN**
Serves **4**

1 Preheat the broiler. Whisk together the eggs, egg whites, cheese, salt, and ground pepper in a medium bowl; set aside.

2 Heat the oil in a 10-inch ovenproof skillet over medium-high heat. Add the onion, garlic, basil, and oregano; cook, stirring occasionally, until the onion softens, 1–2 minutes. Add the asparagus and cook, stirring frequently, until bright green, about 4 minutes. Add the roasted peppers and cook, stirring occasionally, until the asparagus are crisp-tender, about 3 minutes. Add the egg mixture and stir gently to distribute the vegetables evenly in the skillet. Reduce the heat and cook just until the eggs are set in the center, 7–8 minutes (but do not stir).

3 Place the skillet under the broiler and broil the frittata 5 inches from the heat until the top is lightly browned, about 2 minutes. Let stand 5 minutes before serving.

3 large eggs
5 egg whites
¼ cup grated Parmesan cheese
¼ teaspoon salt
⅛ teaspoon freshly ground pepper
1 teaspoon extra-virgin olive oil
1 onion, chopped
3 garlic cloves, minced
1 teaspoon dried basil
1 teaspoon dried oregano
½ pound fresh asparagus, trimmed and cut into 1-inch pieces
1 (7-ounce) jar roasted red peppers (not in oil), drained and chopped

PER SERVING (¼ of frittata): 150 Cal, 7 g Fat, 2 g Sat Fat, 0 g Trans Fat, 163 mg Chol, 429 mg Sod, 11 g Carb, 2 g Fib, 13 g Prot, 121 mg Calc. *POINTS* value: *3.*

Make It Core It's easy to enjoy this frittata if you're following the **Core Plan**—just substitute an extra sprinkling of salt for the Parmesan cheese.

Shirred Eggs with Spinach

༄༅

Hands-On Prep **10 MIN**
Cook **20 MIN**
Serves **4**

1 Preheat the oven to 325°F. Spray 4 (6-ounce) baking dishes with nonstick spray.

2 Heat the oil in a small nonstick skillet over medium-high heat. Add the garlic and cook until fragrant, about 30 seconds. Add the spinach, ⅛ teaspoon of the salt, and ⅛ teaspoon of the pepper. Cook, stirring occasionally, until most of the liquid from the spinach evaporates, about 2 minutes. Divide the spinach mixture among the baking dishes. Carefully break 1 egg into each dish.

3 Place the baking dishes on a small rimmed baking sheet and bake just until the eggs begin to set, about 15 minutes. Sprinkle each egg with 1 teaspoon of the cheese and the remaining ⅛ teaspoon of the salt and pepper. Bake until the egg whites are opaque and the yolks are set, 4–5 minutes. Serve at once.

2 teaspoons extra-virgin olive oil
3 garlic cloves, minced
1 (10-ounce) package frozen chopped spinach, thawed and squeezed dry
¼ teaspoon salt
¼ teaspoon freshly ground pepper
4 large eggs
4 teaspoons grated Parmesan cheese

PER SERVING (1 dish): 123 Cal, 8 g Fat, 2 g Sat Fat, 0 g Trans Fat, 214 mg Chol, 292 mg Sod, 4 g Carb, 2 g Fib, 9 g Prot, 131 mg Calc. **POINTS** value: **3.**

Good Idea Serve this homey egg dish with a side of high-fiber whole-grain toast. A 1-ounce slice with each serving will increase the **POINTS** value by **1.**

Soufflé Omelette with Fruit Compote

─────────── ✿ ───────────

Hands-On Prep **15 MIN**
Cook **15 MIN**
Serves **2**

1 Preheat the oven to 350°F. To make the compote, combine the nectarine, peach, strawberries, 1 tablespoon of the sugar, and the orange juice in a medium saucepan. Cook, stirring occasionally, over medium-high heat, until the fruit softens, about 5 minutes. Set aside and keep warm.

2 With an electric mixer on high speed, beat the egg yolks, 1 tablespoon of the sugar, the vanilla, and cinnamon in a bowl until pale and thick; set aside.

3 With clean beaters and the electric mixer on high speed, beat the egg whites in a bowl until soft peaks form. Gradually add the remaining 3 tablespoons of sugar and beat until stiff peaks form. With a rubber spatula, gently fold the beaten whites, one third at a time, into the yolk mixture, just until blended.

4 Melt the butter in a 10-inch nonstick ovenproof skillet over medium heat. Add the egg mixture, spreading with a spatula, and cook until the sides of the omelette begin to rise, 5–7 minutes. Transfer the skillet to the oven and bake until the top begins to brown, 5–7 minutes. Slide the omelette onto a plate. Spoon the compote evenly over half the omelette and fold the other half over the compote. Serve at once.

1 nectarine, pitted and sliced
1 peach, pitted and sliced
5 fresh strawberries, hulled and sliced
5 tablespoons sugar
3 tablespoons orange juice
2 egg yolks
1 teaspoon vanilla extract
¼ teaspoon cinnamon
4 egg whites
1 teaspoon unsalted butter

PER SERVING (½ of omelette): 299 Cal, 5 g Fat, 2 g Sat Fat, 0 g Trans Fat, 213 mg Chol, 117 mg Sod, 52 g Carb, 4 g Fib, 11 g Prot, 39 mg Calc. ***POINTS*** value: **6.**

CHERRY-CHEESE BLINTZES

Cherry-Cheese Blintzes

⤭

Hands-On Prep **20 MIN**
Cook **20 MIN**
Serves **6**

1 Combine the flour, salt, and nutmeg in a bowl.
Combine the milk and egg. Blend the milk mixture
into the flour mixture; let stand 15 minutes.

2 Bring the cherries, 5 tablespoons of the granulated
sugar, 1 tablespoon water, and the almond extract
to a boil in a small saucepan. Reduce the heat and
simmer until slightly thickened. Whisk together the
cornstarch and 2 teaspoons water in a cup; stir into
the cherry mixture. Return the mixture to a boil and
cook until thickened, about 1 minute. Set aside.

3 Spray a small nonstick skillet with nonstick spray
and set over medium heat. Pour a scant 3 tablespoons
batter onto the skillet and swirl to cover. Cook until
set, 1–2 minutes. Flip and cook through, about
15 seconds. Slide the crêpe onto a plate. Repeat
with the remaining batter to make a total of 6 crêpes.

4 Preheat the oven to 350°F. Spray a baking sheet
with nonstick spray. Combine the cheese, the
remaining granulated sugar, and the vanilla in a
bowl. Spread 4 teaspoons of the cheese mixture on
each crêpe, leaving a 1-inch border. Top the mixture
on each crêpe with 2 tablespoons of the cherry
mixture and roll up. Place the blintzes, seam side
down, on the baking sheet and bake until hot, about
5 minutes. Sprinkle with the confectioners' sugar.

6 tablespoons all-purpose flour
¼ teaspoon salt
⅛ teaspoon ground nutmeg
¾ cup fat-free milk
1 large egg, lightly beaten
1¾ cups frozen pitted tart red cherries
6 tablespoons granulated sugar
¼ teaspoon almond extract
2 teaspoons cornstarch
½ cup pot cheese
¼ teaspoon vanilla extract
1 tablespoon confectioners' sugar

PER SERVING (1 blintz): 157 Cal, 3 g Fat, 1 g Sat Fat, 0 g Trans Fat,
43 mg Chol, 158 mg Sod, 27 g Carb, 1 g Fib, 6 g Prot, 107 mg Calc.
POINTS value: **3.**

Ham-and-Cheese Spoon Bread

ଚ୬

Hands-On Prep **15 MIN**
Cook **1 HR 15 MIN**
Serves **6**

1 Preheat the oven to 375°F. Spray a 1½-quart soufflé or deep baking dish with nonstick spray; coat the bottom and sides with the bread crumbs.

2 Bring the milk, salt, and pepper to a simmer in a large saucepan over medium-high heat. Gradually add the cornmeal, whisking constantly, until blended. Cook, stirring constantly, until the mixture is thick and smooth, about 2 minutes. Transfer to a large bowl and let cool 2 minutes. Stir in the egg yolks and let cool 20 minutes.

3 Melt the butter in a medium nonstick skillet over medium-high heat. Add the onion and garlic; cook, stirring occasionally, until softened. Add the ham and cook until lightly browned, 6–7 minutes. Let stand until slightly cooled, about 5 minutes. Stir the ham mixture and the cheese into the cornmeal mixture; set aside.

4 With an electric mixer on high speed, beat the egg whites in a bowl until stiff peaks form. Gently fold one quarter of the beaten egg whites into the cornmeal mixture until almost combined. Repeat 3 more times. Spoon the batter into the soufflé dish and bake until puffed and golden, 55–60 minutes. Serve at once.

3 tablespoons plain dried bread crumbs
3¼ cups fat-free milk
¾ teaspoon salt
¼ teaspoon freshly ground pepper
1 cup cornmeal
2 egg yolks, lightly beaten
1 tablespoon unsalted butter
1 small onion, chopped
2 garlic cloves, minced
¼ pound lean ham, diced
¼ pound fat-free Swiss cheese, diced
5 egg whites

PER SERVING (about 1 cup): 251 Cal, 5 g Fat, 2 g Sat Fat, 0 g Trans Fat, 84 mg Chol, 901 mg Sod, 30 g Carb, 2 g Fib, 19 g Prot, 275 mg Calc.
POINTS value: **5.**

Banana-Oat Pancakes

❦

Hands-On Prep **10 MIN**
Cook **10 MIN**
Serves **4**

1 Combine the yogurt, egg, egg white, and melted butter in a large bowl. Combine the flour, oats, sugar, baking soda, cinnamon, and salt in another bowl. Add the flour mixture to the yogurt mixture, stirring just until blended. Stir in the banana.

2 Spray a large nonstick skillet or griddle with nonstick spray and set over medium heat. When a drop of water sizzles on it, pour the batter onto it by ¼ cupfuls. Cook just until bubbles begin to appear at the edges of the pancakes, 2–3 minutes. Flip and cook until golden, 2–3 minutes longer. Repeat with the remaining batter, making a total of 8 pancakes.

3 Meanwhile, microwave the jam in a small microwavable dish on High until hot, 1–1½ minutes. Serve at once with the pancakes.

1 (6-ounce) container plain fat-free yogurt
1 large egg, lightly beaten
1 egg white, lightly beaten
1 tablespoon butter, melted
¾ cup all-purpose flour
⅓ cup quick-cooking rolled oats
2 tablespoons sugar
¼ teaspoon baking soda
¼ teaspoon cinnamon
⅛ teaspoon salt
1 ripe banana, sliced
½ cup seedless red raspberry jam

PER SERVING (2 pancakes with 2 tablespoons jam): 329 Cal, 5 g Fat, 2 g Sat Fat, 0 g Trans Fat, 62 mg Chol, 208 mg Sod, 65 g Carb, 2 g Fib, 8 g Prot, 74 mg Calc. *POINTS* value: **7.**

Good Idea Before you begin cooking the pancakes, preheat the oven to 200°F. When each batch is done, place the pancakes in a single layer on a baking sheet and keep them warm in the oven.

Apple-Cheddar Pancakes

❧❧

Hands-On Prep **10 MIN**
Cook **25 MIN**
Serves **6**

1 Melt 2 teaspoons of the butter in a large nonstick skillet over medium-high heat. Add the apple and sugar; cook, stirring occasionally, until the apple is lightly browned, about 5 minutes. Transfer the apple to a small bowl and let cool 5 minutes.

2 Meanwhile, microwave the remaining 3 teaspoons of butter in a microwavable cup on High until melted, 30 seconds. Combine the melted butter, ½ cup of the sour cream, the milk, and egg in a large bowl. Combine the flour, baking powder, and salt in another bowl. Add the flour mixture to the milk mixture, stirring just until blended. Stir in the apples, cheese, chives, and thyme.

3 Wipe out the skillet; spray with nonstick spray and set over medium heat. When a drop of water sizzles on it, pour the batter onto it by ¼ cupfuls. Cook just until bubbles begin to appear at the edges of the pancakes, about 3 minutes. Flip and cook until golden, about 3 minutes longer. Repeat with the remaining batter, making a total of 12 pancakes. Serve at once with the remaining ½ cup of sour cream.

5 teaspoons unsalted butter
1 Golden Delicious apple, peeled and finely chopped
2 teaspoons sugar
1 cup fat-free sour cream
¾ cup fat-free milk
1 large egg, lightly beaten
1⅓ cups all-purpose flour
1½ teaspoons baking powder
¾ teaspoon salt
½ cup shredded reduced-fat sharp cheddar cheese
2 tablespoons chopped fresh chives
1 teaspoon chopped fresh thyme, or ¼ teaspoon dried

PER SERVING (2 pancakes with 4 teaspoons sour cream): 234 Cal, 7 g Fat, 4 g Sat Fat, 0 g Trans Fat, 53 mg Chol, 510 mg Sod, 34 g Carb, 1 g Fib, 9 g Prot, 180 mg Calc. **POINTS** value: **5.**

Food Note A Golden Delicious apple is sweet and cooks beautifully, but if you want to substitute another variety, try a Gala or a pleasantly tart Granny Smith.

Buttermilk Corn Cakes

Hands-On Prep **10 MIN**
Cook **10 MIN**
Serves **4**

1 Combine the flour, cornmeal, sugar, baking powder, baking soda, and salt in a large bowl. Combine the buttermilk and egg in another bowl. Add the buttermilk mixture to the flour mixture, stirring just until blended.

2 Melt 1 teaspoon of the butter in a large nonstick skillet over medium heat. Pour the batter by ¼ cupfuls onto the skillet. Cook just until bubbles begin to appear at the edges of the corn cakes, about 2 minutes. Flip and cook until golden, about 2 minutes longer. Repeat with the remaining butter and batter, making a total of 12 corn cakes. Serve at once with the maple syrup.

PER SERVING (3 corn cakes with 1 tablespoon syrup): 328 Cal, 5 g Fat, 3 g Sat Fat, 0 g Trans Fat, 64 mg Chol, 346 mg Sod, 61 g Carb, 2 g Fib, 9 g Prot, 135 mg Calc. *POINTS* value: **7.**

1 cup all-purpose flour
½ cup cornmeal
2 tablespoons sugar
1 teaspoon baking powder
¼ teaspoon baking soda
⅛ teaspoon salt
1¼ cups low-fat buttermilk
1 large egg, lightly beaten
3 teaspoons unsalted butter
¼ cup warm maple syrup

Zap It To warm up the maple syrup in a jiffy, microwave it in a small microwavable bowl on High 30 to 40 seconds.

Pear Dutch Baby

❧

Hands-On Prep **10 MIN**
Cook **15 MIN**
Serves **4**

1 Preheat the oven to 425°F. Combine the flour, sugar, and nutmeg in a large bowl. Combine the eggs, egg whites, and milk in another bowl. Add the egg mixture to the flour mixture, stirring just until blended.

2 Put the 1 tablespoon of butter in a 10-inch ovenproof skillet. Place the skillet in the oven until the butter melts, about 2 minutes. Remove the skillet from the oven and swirl so that the butter covers the skillet. Pour the batter into the hot skillet, return it to the oven, and bake until the pancake is puffed and browned, about 15 minutes.

3 Meanwhile, to make the topping, melt the additional 2 teaspoons butter in a medium nonstick skillet over medium-high heat. Add the pears and cook until crisp-tender, 2–3 minutes. Stir in the remaining ingredients; cook, stirring, until the pears are tender, 2–3 minutes.

4 Spoon the topping onto the pancake and cut the pancake into 4 wedges. Serve at once.

- **1 cup all-purpose flour**
- **2 tablespoons sugar**
- **⅛ teaspoon ground nutmeg**
- **2 large eggs, lightly beaten**
- **2 egg whites, lightly beaten**
- **¾ cup fat-free milk**
- **1 tablespoon + 2 teaspoons unsalted butter**
- **2 pears, peeled and sliced**
- **2 tablespoons honey**
- **½ teaspoon vanilla extract**
- **¼ teaspoon cinnamon**

PER SERVING (1 wedge with about ½ cup topping): 291 Cal, 8 g Fat, 4 g Sat Fat, 0 g Trans Fat, 120 mg Chol, 60 mg Sod, 48 g Carb, 2 g Fib, 8 g Prot, 79 mg Calc. *POINTS* value: **6.**

Food Note A heavy-bottomed cast-iron skillet is ideal for baking this pancake, but if you don't have one, use any kind of ovenproof skillet or use a non-ovenproof skillet and wrap the handle in heavy-duty foil.

PEAR DUTCH BABY

Buttermilk Whole-Grain Waffles

❧

Hands-On Prep **10 MIN**
Cook **PER WAFFLE BAKER DIRECTIONS**
Serves **8**

1 Preheat a waffle baker according to the manufacturer's directions.

2 Meanwhile, combine the all-purpose and whole-wheat flours, the cornmeal, sugar, baking powder, baking soda, and salt in a large bowl. Combine the buttermilk, eggs, egg whites, and melted butter in another bowl. Add the buttermilk mixture to the flour mixture, stirring until well blended.

3 When the waffle baker is ready, pour the batter onto the center and quickly spread to within 1 inch of the edges. Close the baker and bake as the manufacturer directs; do not open until done. Repeat, reheating the waffle baker before adding each batch of batter. Serve waffles at once with the honey.

¾ cup all-purpose flour
½ cup whole-wheat flour
¼ cup cornmeal
3 tablespoons sugar
1 teaspoon baking powder
½ teaspoon baking soda
¼ teaspoon salt
1¾ cups low-fat buttermilk
2 large eggs, lightly beaten
2 egg whites, lightly beaten
1 tablespoon unsalted butter, melted
½ cup honey

PER SERVING (a 4-inch square waffle with 1 teaspoon honey): 209 Cal, 3 g Fat, 2 g Sat Fat, 0 g Trans Fat, 59 mg Chol, 191 mg Sod, 43 g Carb, 2 g Fib, 7 g Prot, 57 mg Calc. *POINTS* value: *4.*

Good Idea While cooking the waffles, keep each batch warm in a 200°F oven. Place the cooked waffles in a single layer directly on the oven rack so that they'll remain crisp.

Peanut-Butter French Toast

Hands-On Prep **15 MIN**
Cook **10 MIN**
Serves **4**

1 Spread each of 4 slices of bread with 1 teaspoon of the peanut butter and top with the remaining 4 slices of bread. Prick both sides of each sandwich a few times with a fork.

2 Combine the egg substitute, sugar, and vanilla in a large shallow bowl. Add a sandwich and let it stand until evenly soaked on each side, about 30 seconds per side. Transfer to a plate. Repeat with the remaining sandwiches.

3 Melt 1 teaspoon of the butter in a large nonstick skillet over medium-high heat. Add 2 of the sandwiches and cook until browned, 2–3 minutes on each side. Repeat with the remaining 2 sandwiches. Cut each sandwich in half and serve at once with the jam.

8 very thin slices whole-wheat bread
8 teaspoons reduced-fat peanut butter
¾ cup fat-free egg substitute
1 tablespoon sugar
1 teaspoon vanilla extract
2 teaspoons unsalted butter
4 tablespoons strawberry or raspberry jam

PER SERVING (2 sandwich halves with 1 tablespoon jam): 287 Cal, 8 g Fat, 2 g Sat Fat, 0 g Trans Fat, 5 mg Chol, 417 mg Sod, 44 g Carb, 2 g Fib, 13 g Prot, 56 mg Calc. *POINTS* value: *6.*

Plan Ahead Get a jump-start on breakfast by preparing the sandwiches as directed through step 2; then cover with plastic wrap and refrigerate overnight. Follow step 3 in the morning, and you'll have a yummy hot breakfast in no time flat.

Cinnamon-Raisin "Bruschetta" with Strawberries

Hands-On Prep **10 MIN**
Cook **2 MIN**
Serves **4**

1 Combine the strawberries, sugar, lemon zest, and lemon juice in a small bowl. Let stand, stirring occasionally, until the sugar dissolves, about 10 minutes.

2 Meanwhile, combine the cream cheese, honey, and vanilla in another small bowl.

3 Toast the bread and cool slightly, about 30 seconds. Spread the cream cheese mixture on the bread. Cut each slice into 4 squares. Top each slice of "bruschetta" with about 2 teaspoons of the strawberry mixture and serve at once.

PER SERVING (4 squares): 147 Cal, 4 g Fat, 1 g Sat Fat, 0 g Trans Fat, 6 mg Chol, 162 mg Sod, 25 g Carb, 2 g Fib, 4 g Prot, 41 mg Calc. *POINTS* value: **3.**

8 large fresh strawberries, hulled and finely chopped
1½ tablespoons sugar
½ teaspoon grated lemon zest
2 teaspoons fresh lemon juice
3 tablespoons light soft cream cheese
2 teaspoons honey
¼ teaspoon vanilla extract
4 slices cinnamon-raisin bread

Food Note For this recipe we like to use light soft cream cheese, the kind that comes in a tub, because it's spreadable straight from the fridge. If you don't have any, substitute an equal amount of light cream cheese (Neufchâtel) from a bar. Just allow it to soften at room temperature, about 15 minutes, before spreading.

Date and Almond Oatmeal

Hands-On Prep **10 MIN**
Cook **35 MIN**
Serves **4**

1 Bring the water to a boil in a large saucepan. Add the oats and salt; cook at a low boil, stirring occasionally, until mixture begins to thicken, about 10 minutes. Reduce the heat and simmer until very thick, about 15 minutes. Stir in the dates, the 3 tablespoons of honey, and the vanilla; simmer, stirring occasionally, until the oats are tender, 12–15 minutes longer.

2 Meanwhile, place the almonds in a small nonstick skillet over medium-high heat. Cook, shaking the skillet often, until lightly browned, 3–4 minutes. Set the almonds aside.

3 Divide the oatmeal among 4 bowls. Top evenly with the almonds and the additional 4 teaspoons honey. Serve at once.

- **4 cups water**
- **1 cup steel-cut oats**
- **¼ teaspoon salt**
- **¾ cup pitted dates, quartered**
- **3 tablespoons + 4 teaspoons honey**
- **1½ teaspoons vanilla extract**
- **¼ cup sliced almonds**

PER SERVING (¾ cup oatmeal with 1 tablespoon almonds and 1 teaspoon honey): 346 Cal, 6 g Fat, 1 g Sat Fat, 0 g Trans Fat, 0 mg Chol, 148 mg Sod, 71 g Carb, 7 g Fib, 8 g Prot, 50 mg Calc. *POINTS* value: **7.**

Try It Steel-cut oats are groats (the inner portion of the oat kernel) that have been cut into 2 or 3 pieces using steel disks. These golden-colored oats resemble tiny rice particles. Unlike rolled oats, steel-cut oats undergo no additional processing, so they're prized for their natural taste and chewy texture.

OATMEAL WITH
FRESH BERRY SAUCE

Oatmeal with Fresh Berry Sauce

Hands-On Prep **5 MIN**
Cook **8 MIN**
Serves **2**

✓

1 Bring the blueberries, raspberries, and water to a boil in a small saucepan over medium heat. Cook, stirring occasionally, until the mixture thickens slightly, 3–4 minutes. Remove the pan from the heat; stir in the orange zest and vanilla. Set aside.

2 Bring the milk, salt, and cinnamon to a boil in another small saucepan. Add the oatmeal; reduce the heat and cook, stirring occasionally, until thickened, about 1 minute.

3 Divide the oatmeal between 2 bowls. Spoon half the berry sauce into each bowl and serve at once.

½ **cup fresh blueberries**
½ **cup fresh raspberries**
 3 **tablespoons water**
½ **teaspoon grated**
   orange zest
¼ **teaspoon vanilla extract**
 1 **cup fat-free milk**
⅛ **teaspoon salt**
⅛ **teaspoon cinnamon**
 1 **cup uncooked instant**
   oatmeal

PER SERVING (generous ¾ cup oatmeal with ⅓ cup sauce):
229 Cal, 3 g Fat, 1 g Sat Fat, 0 g Trans Fat, 3 mg Chol, 529 mg Sod, 40 g Carb, 7 g Fib, 10 g Prot, 402 mg Calc. *POINTS* value: **4.**

Food Note Frozen berries work beautifully in this recipe too. Just reduce the water to 1–2 tablespoons and allow a few extra minutes of cooking time for the berry sauce to thicken in step 1.

Orange-Cranberry Scones

⸙

Hands-On Prep **15 MIN**
Cook **20 MIN**
Serves **12**

1 Preheat the oven to 350°F. Spray a large baking sheet with nonstick spray.

2 Combine the all-purpose flour, whole-wheat flour, sugar, baking powder, baking soda, and salt in a large bowl. With a pastry blender, cut in the butter until the mixture is crumbly. Stir in the cranberries.

3 Put 2 tablespoons of the buttermilk in a cup and set aside. Combine the remaining buttermilk, the egg, and orange zest in a small bowl. Add the buttermilk mixture to the flour mixture, stirring with a wooden spoon just until moistened. Knead the mixture in the bowl once or twice to form a ball. On a lightly floured surface, pat the dough into a 10 x 6-inch rectangle. Cut into 12 (2½ x 2-inch) pieces with a large knife.

4 Place the pieces on the baking sheet; brush the tops with the reserved 2 tablespoons of buttermilk. Bake until a toothpick inserted into a scone comes out clean, 20–22 minutes. Transfer the scones to a rack and let cool 5 minutes. Serve warm or let cool completely.

1½ cups all-purpose flour
½ cup whole-wheat flour
½ cup sugar
1½ teaspoons baking powder
½ teaspoon baking soda
¼ teaspoon salt
4 tablespoons cold unsalted butter, cut into small pieces
¾ cup sweetened dried cranberries
¾ cup low-fat buttermilk
1 large egg, lightly beaten
1 teaspoon grated orange zest

PER SERVING (1 scone): 175 Cal, 5 g Fat, 3 g Sat Fat, 0 g Trans Fat, 29 mg Chol, 171 mg Sod, 31 g Carb, 1 g Fib, 3 g Prot, 35 mg Calc.
POINTS value: *4.*

Good Idea Substitute an equal amount of your favorite dried fruit for the cranberries—perhaps raisins or chopped apricots, dried plums, apples, or pears.

Blueberry-Ginger Corn Muffins

───────── ❧ ─────────

Hands-On Prep **15 MIN**
Cook **15 MIN**
Serves **12**

1 Preheat the oven to 425°F. Spray a 12-cup muffin tin with nonstick spray.

2 Combine the flour, cornmeal, sugar, baking powder, and salt in a large bowl. Combine the milk, oil, and egg in another bowl. Add the milk mixture to the flour mixture, stirring just until blended. Gently fold in the blueberries and ginger.

3 Spoon the batter into the cups, filling each cup about two thirds full. Bake until a toothpick inserted into a muffin comes out clean, 12–15 minutes. Immediately remove the muffins from the pan and cool completely on a rack.

1 cup all-purpose flour
¾ cup cornmeal
½ cup sugar
2 teaspoons baking powder
¼ teaspoon salt
½ cup fat-free milk
¼ cup corn oil
1 large egg, lightly beaten
1 cup frozen blueberries
3 tablespoons chopped
  crystallized ginger

PER SERVING (1 muffin): 176 Cal, 5 g Fat, 1 g Sat Fat, 0 g Trans Fat, 18 mg Chol, 124 mg Sod, 30 g Carb, 1 g Fib, 3 g Prot, 35 mg Calc.
POINTS value: *4.*

Plan Ahead These muffins freeze beautifully, so bake an extra batch. Cool as directed; then wrap each muffin in plastic wrap. Transfer the muffins to a large zip-close plastic bag and freeze up to 1 month. The individual wrapping makes it easy to grab just a muffin or two as you need them.

Fresh and Simple Salads

CHAPTER 3

GREEN GODDESS COBB SALAD

Green Goddess Cobb Salad

Hands-On Prep **20 MIN**
Cook **NONE**
Serves **4**

1 To make the dressing, put the yogurt, mayonnaise, parsley, chives, scallion, vinegar, salt, and pepper in a blender and pulse until smooth.

2 Scatter the lettuce and arugula over a platter. Top with neat rows of the turkey, egg whites, avocado, tomatoes, and bacon.

3 Drizzle half the dressing over the salad and serve at once, with the remaining dressing on the side.

PER SERVING (1½ cups with about 2 tablespoons dressing): 224 Cal, 8 g Fat, 2 g Sat Fat, 0 g Trans Fat, 56 mg Chol, 580 mg Sod, 12 g Carb, 3 g Fib, 26 g Prot, 110 mg Calc. **POINTS** value: **5.**

Try It We prefer Hass avocados for this recipe, the avocados with the distinctive black pebbly skin. Hass avocados contain slightly more fat than the smaller green-skinned types, which are grown in Florida, but their buttery taste and velvety texture justify their few extra calories.

½ cup plain fat-free yogurt
¼ cup fat-free mayonnaise
½ cup chopped fresh parsley
¼ cup chopped fresh chives
1 scallion, chopped
1 teaspoon red-wine vinegar
¼ teaspoon salt
⅛ teaspoon freshly ground pepper
½ small head iceberg lettuce, chopped (about 3 cups)
1 bunch arugula, chopped (about 1 cup)
½ pound skinless cooked turkey breast, sliced
3 hard-cooked egg whites, chopped
½ medium Hass avocado, pitted, peeled, and chopped
2 tomatoes, seeded and chopped
4 crisp-cooked turkey-bacon slices, coarsely chopped

Classic Chef's Salad

❧❦

Hands-On Prep **15 MIN**
Cook **NONE**
Serves **4**

1 To make the dressing, whisk together the mayonnaise, yogurt, ketchup, and ground pepper in a salad bowl.

2 Add the lettuce and cucumber to the dressing; toss to coat evenly. Arrange the bell pepper, tomato, chicken, cheese, and egg on top of the salad in an attractive pattern and serve at once.

PER SERVING (2½ cups): 139 Cal, 7 g Fat, 2 g Sat Fat, 0 g Trans Fat, 66 mg Chol, 289 mg Sod, 10 g Carb, 2 g Fib, 12 g Prot, 244 mg Calc. **POINTS** value: **3.**

Make It Core If you're following the **Core Plan**, make the dressing as directed but use fat-free mayonnaise and replace the reduced-fat Swiss cheese with a fat-free cheese.

2 tablespoons reduced-calorie mayonnaise
¼ cup plain fat-free yogurt
2 tablespoons ketchup
Freshly ground pepper, to taste
1 head romaine lettuce, torn into bite-size pieces (6 cups)
1 cucumber, peeled and sliced
1 yellow bell pepper, seeded and sliced into thin rings
1 tomato, cut into 8 wedges
2 ounces reduced-sodium chicken breast, cut into matchstick-thin strips
2 ounces reduced-fat Swiss cheese, cut into matchstick-thin strips
1 large hard-cooked egg, quartered

Poached Egg and Spring Greens Salad

⟡⟡

Hands-On Prep **10 MIN**
Cook **10 MIN**
Serves **4**

☑

1 To make the dressing, combine the shallot, mustard, white-wine vinegar, salt, and pepper in a large bowl. Set aside.

2 Spread paper towels on a large plate. Bring 2 inches of water just to a boil in a large skillet; stir in the white vinegar. Reduce the heat to a very gentle simmer. One at a time, break the eggs into a saucer and then slip them into the skillet. Cook until the whites are set and the yolks begin to thicken but have not hardened, 2–3 minutes. With a slotted spoon, transfer the eggs, one at a time, to the plate and drain on the paper towels.

3 Add the greens to the dressing in the bowl; toss to coat. Divide among 4 plates. Top each salad with an egg and serve at once.

1 small shallot, finely chopped
1 tablespoon Dijon mustard
1 tablespoon white-wine vinegar
¼ teaspoon salt
⅛ teaspoon freshly ground pepper
2 tablespoons white vinegar
4 large eggs
8 cups mixed baby greens

PER SERVING (about 2 cups with 1 egg): 103 Cal, 6 g Fat, 2 g Sat Fat, 0 g Trans Fat, 213 mg Chol, 332 mg Sod, 6 g Carb, 3 g Fib, 8 g Prot, 93 mg Calc. **POINTS** value: *2.*

Zap It To poach the eggs in the microwave, pour ⅔ cup water into a 1-quart microwavable bowl or baking dish. Break and slip in the eggs. Gently prick the yolks with a toothpick. Cover the bowl with plastic wrap and microwave on High 1½ to 2 minutes. Let stand, covered, until the whites are completely set and the yolks begin to thicken but have not hardened, 1 to 2 minutes. Transfer to paper towels to drain.

Tossed Greek Salad

Hands-On Prep **15 MIN**
Cook **NONE**
Serves **4**

1 To make the dressing, combine the broth, oil, vinegar, oregano, garlic, salt, and ground pepper in a small bowl. Let stand until the flavors are blended, about 5 minutes. Discard the garlic clove.

2 Meanwhile, combine the lettuce, cucumber, bell pepper, tomato, dill, and olives in a large bowl. Pour the dressing over the salad; toss to coat. Top with the anchovies, sprinkle with the cheese, and serve at once.

PER SERVING (2½ cups): 128 Cal, 10 g Fat, 4 g Sat Fat, 0 g Trans Fat, 17 mg Chol, 449 mg Sod, 7 g Carb, 3 g Fib, 4 g Prot, 134 mg Calc. **POINTS** value: **3**.

Make It Core If you're following the **Core Plan**, skip the anchovies and use fat-free feta cheese.

¼ cup reduced-sodium vegetable broth
4 teaspoons olive oil
1 tablespoon red-wine vinegar
1½ teaspoons dried oregano
1 garlic clove, bruised
¼ teaspoon salt
¼ teaspoon freshly ground pepper
1 head red-leaf lettuce, torn into bite-size pieces (6 cups)
1 cucumber, peeled, seeded, and chopped
1 green bell pepper, seeded and cut into ½-inch strips
1 tomato, cut into 8 wedges
¼ cup chopped fresh dill
10 small black olives, pitted and sliced
4 anchovies, rinsed and chopped
½ cup crumbled feta cheese

Warm Spinach, Mushroom, and Bacon Salad

※

Hands-On Prep **10 MIN**
Cook **15 MIN**
Serves **6**

1 Place the spinach and mushrooms in a salad bowl; set aside.

2 Heat the oil in a large nonstick skillet over medium heat. Add the broth, red onion, orange zest, orange juice, vinegar, and salt. Cook, stirring occasionally, until the onions are very tender and the liquid has thickened and reduced to ½ cup, about 15 minutes. Remove the skillet from the heat; let stand until the dressing cools slightly, about 10 minutes.

3 Pour the warm dressing over the spinach and mushrooms; toss to coat. Sprinkle with the bacon pieces and pepper. Serve at once.

PER SERVING (2 cups): 86 Cal, 5 g Fat, 1 g Sat Fat, 0 g Trans Fat, 1 mg Chol, 238 mg Sod, 8 g Carb, 2 g Fib, 3 g Prot, 58 mg Calc. **POINTS** value: **2.**

Express Lane Use 8 cups baby spinach, and you won't have to stem it and tear it into bite-size pieces.

1 (10-ounce) bag triple-washed fresh spinach, torn into bite-size pieces
1 (10-ounce) package sliced fresh mushrooms
2 tablespoons olive oil
2 cups reduced-sodium vegetable broth
1 red onion, thinly sliced and separated into rings
1 teaspoon grated orange zest
¼ cup fresh orange juice
2 tablespoons apple-cider vinegar
¼ teaspoon salt
1 crisp-cooked bacon slice, crumbled
¼ teaspoon freshly ground pepper

Our Best Caesar Salad

❧

Hands-On Prep **10 MIN**
Cook **NONE**
Serves **4**

1 Rub a large salad bowl with the garlic clove. Add the broth, oil, lemon juice, mustard, anchovy paste, and pepper; whisk until blended. Let stand until the flavors are blended, about 5 minutes.

2 Discard the garlic. Add the lettuce to the bowl and toss to coat. Sprinkle with the croutons and Parmesan cheese. Serve at once.

PER SERVING (2 cups): 94 Cal, 6 g Fat, 1 g Sat Fat, 0 g Trans Fat, 4 mg Chol, 184 mg Sod, 6 g Carb, 2 g Fib, 4 g Prot, 83 mg Calc. *POINTS* value: *2.*

How We Did It We find that bruising garlic helps to release its flavor. To bruise garlic, place a peeled clove on a cutting board and flatten it slightly with the side of a large knife.

1 large garlic clove, bruised
¼ cup reduced-sodium chicken broth
4 teaspoons extra-virgin olive oil
1 tablespoon fresh lemon juice
1 teaspoon Dijon mustard
¾ teaspoon anchovy paste
¼ teaspoon freshly ground pepper
1 head romaine lettuce, torn into bite-size pieces (6 cups)
1 cup fat-free croutons
2 tablespoons grated Parmesan cheese

Arugula-Pear Salad with Blue Cheese Dressing

Hands-On Prep **15 MIN**
Cook **NONE**
Serves **4**

1 To make the dressing, combine the cheese, broth, oil, vinegar, garlic, and pepper in a small bowl. Let stand until the flavors are blended, at least 5 minutes.

2 Meanwhile, combine the pear and lemon juice in a small bowl; toss to coat. Arrange the arugula and pear slices on a platter.

3 Discard the garlic clove. Drizzle the dressing over the salad and serve at once.

PER SERVING (1½ cups): 115 Cal, 8 g Fat, 3 g Sat Fat, 0 g Trans Fat, 11 mg Chol, 182 mg Sod, 8 g Carb, 1 g Fib, 3 g Prot, 97 mg Calc. **POINTS** value: **3.**

⅓ **cup crumbled blue cheese**
¼ **cup reduced-sodium vegetable broth**
4 **teaspoons extra-virgin olive oil**
1 **tablespoon apple-cider vinegar**
1 **garlic clove, bruised**
¼ **teaspoon freshly ground pepper**
1 **pear, thinly sliced**
1 **tablespoon fresh lemon juice**
1 **bunch arugula, cleaned**

Try It If you love blue cheese, consider using *Gorgonzola* (gawr-guhn-ZOH-lah), for its rich and slightly pungent flavor in this salad. Look for an ivory-colored interior streaked with bluish-green veins. Gorgonzola usually comes wrapped in foil to keep it moist. Refrigerated and carefully wrapped, it will keep well for several weeks.

Mesclun with Roasted Beets and Cheese Croûtes

❧

Hands-On Prep **20 MIN**
Cook **25 MIN**
Serves **4**

1 Preheat the oven to 400°F. Spray a small baking pan with nonstick spray. Combine the beets and thyme in the pan; toss to coat and spray the beets with nonstick spray. Roast, stirring occasionally, until tender, about 25 minutes. Let cool.

2 Meanwhile, to make the croûtes, spread the toasted bread with the goat cheese; sprinkle with the parsley and set aside.

3 To make the dressing, combine the broth, oil, vinegar, mustard, garlic clove, salt, and pepper in a large bowl; let stand 2 minutes, then discard the garlic. Whisk until smooth.

4 To assemble the salad, drizzle 1 teaspoon of the dressing over the beets in the pan and toss to coat. Add the greens to the bowl with the remaining dressing and toss to coat. Divide the greens among 4 plates. Top each serving with one fourth of the beets and a croûte. Serve at once.

2 fresh beets, peeled, trimmed, and cubed
1 teaspoon chopped fresh thyme
4 (1-ounce) slices toasted French bread
2 ounces goat cheese
2 tablespoons chopped flat-leaf parsley
3 tablespoons reduced-sodium chicken broth
4 teaspoons olive oil
2 teaspoons white-wine vinegar
1 teaspoon Dijon mustard
1 garlic clove, bruised
¼ teaspoon salt
¼ teaspoon freshly ground pepper
½ pound mesclun greens

PER SERVING (2 cups with 1 croûte): 199 Cal, 9 g Fat, 3 g Sat Fat, 0 g Trans Fat, 13 mg Chol, 437 mg Sod, 21 g Carb, 3 g Fib, 7 g Prot, 163 mg Calc. *POINTS* value: *4.*

Express Lane If you want to serve this salad in a flash, prepare the beets as directed in step 1 and refrigerate in an airtight container up to 2 days or just use canned beets and begin with step 2.

MESCLUN WITH ROASTED
BEETS AND CHEESE CROÛTES

Pasta Salad with Pesto and Tomatoes

Hands-On Prep **15 MIN**
Cook **30 MIN**
Serves **4**

1 Preheat the oven to 400°F. Place the tomato halves, cut side up, in a medium shallow baking dish; drizzle with 1 tablespoon of the oil. Roast until slightly browned on top but still firm, about 20 minutes. Let cool.

2 To make the pesto, put the basil, cheese, pine nuts, the remaining 1 tablespoon of oil, and the pepper in a food processor and pulse, scraping once with a rubber spatula, until the mixture has formed a coarse, bright green paste.

3 Meanwhile, cook the penne according to package directions, omitting the salt if desired. Drain, reserving 1½ tablespoons of the cooking water, and transfer to a large serving bowl. Stir the cooking water into the pesto; add to the penne and toss to coat. Arrange the roasted tomatoes on top. Let cool to room temperature before serving.

8 small plum tomatoes, halved lengthwise
2 tablespoons olive oil
2 cups packed fresh basil leaves
2 tablespoons grated Asiago cheese
1 tablespoon pine nuts
¼ teaspoon freshly ground pepper
2 cups penne

PER SERVING (1 cup pasta with 2 tomato halves): 280 Cal, 10 g Fat, 2 g Sat Fat, 0 g Trans Fat, 2 mg Chol, 70 mg Sod, 40 g Carb, 3 g Fib, 9 g Prot, 90 mg Calc. *POINTS* value: *6.*

Plan Ahead Make extra pesto to have on hand. Freeze it in ice-cube trays until solid. Then transfer the cubes to a zip-close plastic freezer bag and freeze up to 3 months.

Three-Bean Salad with Lemon and Basil

❧

Hands-On Prep **15 MIN**
Cook **15 MIN**
Serves **6**

☑

1 Cook the edamame according to package directions. Rinse in a colander under cold running water; drain.

2 Combine lemon zest, lemon juice, oil, salt, and ground pepper in a medium bowl. Add the edamame, black and white beans, red onion, bell pepper, and basil; toss to coat.

PER SERVING (¾ cup): 160 Cal, 3 g Fat, 0 g Sat Fat, 0 g Trans Fat, 0 mg Chol, 427 mg Sod, 26 g Carb, 8 g Fib, 9 g Prot, 94 mg Calc. **POINTS** value: *3.*

Plan Ahead Unlike the beans in a typical three-bean salad, the beans in this salad won't turn drab olive green when stored. If you make the salad ahead, transfer to an airtight container and refrigerate up to 2 days, but don't add the basil until the last minute.

⅔ cup shelled fresh or frozen edamame (green soybeans)

1 teaspoon grated lemon zest

1½ tablespoons fresh lemon juice

1 tablespoon olive oil

½ teaspoon salt

¼ teaspoon freshly ground pepper

1 (15-ounce) can black beans, rinsed and drained

1 (15-ounce) can small white beans, rinsed and drained

½ small red onion, finely diced

½ small yellow bell pepper, seeded and finely diced

5 large fresh basil leaves, thinly sliced

SPEEDY HOPPIN' JOHN SALAD

Speedy Hoppin' John Salad

Hands-On Prep **10 MIN**
Cook **NONE**
Serves **4**

Combine the peas, bell peppers, celery, red onion, vinegar, oil, thyme, salt, and ground pepper in a large bowl. Serve at once or refrigerate, covered, with plastic wrap overnight.

PER SERVING (1 cup): 100 Cal, 3 g Fat, 0 g Sat Fat, 0 g Trans Fat, 0 mg Chol, 297 mg Sod, 16 g Carb, 4 g Fib, 4 g Prot, 34 mg Calc. **POINTS** value: *1.*

Good Idea Hoppin' John is a Southern dish traditionally prepared on New Year's Day for good luck. Broiled pork chops make a great accompaniment. A 2-ounce cooked boneless loin chop for each serving will increase the **POINTS** value by **3.**

1 (15-ounce) can black-eyed peas, rinsed and drained
1 red bell pepper, seeded and chopped
1 green bell pepper, seeded and chopped
2 celery stalks, chopped
1 small red onion, chopped
2 tablespoons apple-cider vinegar
2 teaspoons olive oil
¼ teaspoon dried thyme
¼ teaspoon salt
¼ teaspoon freshly ground pepper

Simple Tabbouleh

Hands-On Prep **15 MIN**
Cook **5 MIN**
Serves **4**

☑

1 Bring the water to a boil in a small saucepan. Stir in the bulgur and remove the pan from the heat. Cover and let stand until the water is absorbed, about 15 minutes.

2 Fluff the bulgur with a fork; transfer to a medium bowl. Stir in the tomatoes, parsley, cilantro, lemon juice, oil, garlic, salt, and pepper. Serve at once or cover and refrigerate up to 3 days.

PER SERVING (1 cup): 174 Cal, 4 g Fat, 1 g Sat Fat, 0 g Trans Fat, 0 mg Chol, 302 mg Sod, 32 g Carb, 7 g Fib, 5 g Prot, 31 mg Calc. **POINTS** value: **3.**

Good Idea Sprinkle the top of this classic Middle Eastern salad with 1 cup crumbled fat-free feta cheese; the per-serving **POINTS** value will increase by **1.**

- 1 cup water
- 1 cup bulgur
- 2 tomatoes, chopped
- ¼ cup chopped fresh parsley
- ¼ cup chopped fresh cilantro
- ¼ cup fresh lemon juice
- 1 tablespoon extra-virgin olive oil
- 1 garlic clove, minced
- ½ teaspoon salt
- ¼ teaspoon freshly ground pepper

Fragrant Cauliflower and Broccoli Salad

—— ❧ ——

Hands-On Prep **15 MIN**
Cook **20 MIN**
Serves **4**   ☑

1 Bring a large pot of lightly salted water to a boil.
Add the cauliflower and return to a boil; cook
3 minutes. Add the broccoli and cook until the
vegetables are crisp-tender, about 2 minutes. Rinse
in a colander under cold running water; drain well.

2 Heat the oil in a large nonstick skillet over medium-
high heat. Add the vegetables and cook, stirring
frequently, until heated through, about 1 minute. Stir
in the salt, cumin, coriander, cinnamon, and cayenne.
Cook, stirring constantly, until the vegetables are
heated through, 1–2 minutes. Remove the skillet
from the heat; stir in the vinegar, red onion, and
orange zest. Transfer the salad to a bowl and let cool
10 minutes before serving.

PER SERVING (1½ cups): 90 Cal, 4 g Fat, 1 g Sat Fat, 0 g Trans Fat,
0 mg Chol, 545 mg Sod, 11 g Carb, 6 g Fib, 5 g Prot, 54 mg Calc.
POINTS value: **1**.

- **4 cups fresh cauliflower florets**
- **4 cups fresh broccoli florets**
- **1 tablespoon extra-virgin olive oil**
- **½ teaspoon salt**
- **½ teaspoon ground cumin**
- **¼ teaspoon ground coriander**
- **⅛ teaspoon cinnamon**
- **⅛ teaspoon cayenne**
- **1½ tablespoons sherry vinegar**
- **1 small red onion, thinly sliced**
- **1 teaspoon grated orange zest**

Good Idea This salad is also delicious when the
vegetables are roasted. Preheat the oven to 425°F.
Combine the first 8 ingredients in a large bowl; place
equal amounts of the vegetables on 2 large rimmed
baking sheets. Roast, stirring once halfway through
the cooking time, until lightly browned and tender,
about 25 minutes. Return to the bowl and toss with
the remaining ingredients.

Four-Tomato and Basil Salad

❧

Hands-On Prep **10 MIN**
Cook **NONE**
Serves **4**

☑

Combine the tomatoes, basil, vinegar, capers, oil, salt, and pepper in a large bowl. Serve at once or let stand at room temperature up to 30 minutes.

PER SERVING (1½ cups): 105 Cal, 4 g Fat, 1 g Sat Fat, 0 g Trans Fat, 0 mg Chol, 404 mg Sod, 15 g Carb, 3 g Fib, 3 g Prot, 32 mg Calc. **POINTS** value: **2.**

Good Idea For a real summer treat, spoon these tomatoes over a platter lined with sliced fat-free mozzarella cheese. A ¾-ounce slice of fat-free cheese will increase the per-serving **POINTS** value by **1.**

2 tomatoes, each cut into 6 wedges

2 yellow tomatoes, each cut into 6 wedges

2 cups cherry tomatoes, halved

2 cups grape tomatoes, halved

¼ cup thinly sliced fresh basil

1 tablespoon balsamic vinegar

1 tablespoon drained capers

1 tablespoon extra-virgin olive oil

½ teaspoon salt

⅛ teaspoon freshly ground pepper

Fennel, Orange, and Red Cabbage Salad

~~~~~~

Hands-On Prep **15 MIN**
Cook **NONE**
Serves **4**

Whisk together the wine, orange zest, orange juice, oil, honey, lemon juice, vinegars, salt, and pepper in a large salad bowl. Add the cabbage, fennel, and oranges; toss to coat. Serve at once.

PER SERVING (2 cups): 133 Cal, 5 g Fat, 1 g Sat Fat, 0 g Trans Fat, 0 mg Chol, 201 mg Sod, 23 g Carb, 5 g Fib, 3 g Prot, 100 mg Calc. **POINTS** value: **2.**

Express Lane Cut the prep time by using packaged shredded red cabbage. You'll need 4 cups for this recipe.

2 tablespoons dry white wine
1 teaspoon grated orange zest
2 tablespoons fresh orange juice
4 teaspoons extra-virgin olive oil
1 tablespoon honey
1 teaspoon fresh lemon juice
1 teaspoon apple-cider vinegar
1 teaspoon raspberry vinegar
1 teaspoon balsamic vinegar
¼ teaspoon salt
¼ teaspoon freshly ground pepper
1 (1-pound) red cabbage, shredded
1 fennel bulb, trimmed and thinly sliced
2 oranges, peeled, sliced, and cut into bite-size pieces

Time for Soup

MEATBALL AND BARLEY SOUP

Meatball and Barley Soup

❧❧

Hands-On Prep **20 MIN**
Cook **45 MIN**
Serves **4**

☑

1 To make the meatballs, combine the beef, basil,
¼ teaspoon of the salt, and ⅛ teaspoon of the
pepper in a medium bowl. Form into 16 balls. Heat
1 teaspoon of the oil in a large nonstick skillet over
medium-high heat. Add the meatballs and cook,
turning, until browned, about 4 minutes. Set aside.

2 Heat the remaining 1 teaspoon of oil in a large
saucepan over medium-high heat. Add the leeks,
carrots, garlic, and thyme. Cook, stirring occasionally,
until the vegetables begin to soften, 3–4 minutes.
Add the mushrooms and cook, stirring occasionally,
until they begin to release their liquid and the
vegetables soften, 3–4 minutes. Stir in the broth,
tomato paste, and the remaining ¼ teaspoon of salt
and ⅛ teaspoon of pepper; bring to a boil. Reduce
the heat and simmer, covered, until the mushrooms
are tender, about 10 minutes. Stir in the barley and
cook, covered, until almost tender, about 10 minutes.
Add the meatballs and cook, covered, until heated
through, about 5 minutes.

**½ pound ground lean beef
    (5% fat or less)**
¾ teaspoon dried basil
½ teaspoon salt
**¼ teaspoon freshly
    ground pepper**
**2 teaspoons extra-virgin
    olive oil**
**2 large leeks, cleaned and
    chopped (white and light
    green parts only)**
2 carrots, chopped
5 garlic cloves, sliced
½ teaspoon dried thyme
**½ (10-ounce) package fresh
    mushrooms, sliced**
**2 (14½-ounce) cans
    reduced-sodium
    beef broth**
¼ cup tomato paste
⅓ cup quick-cooking barley

PER SERVING (1½ cups soup with 4 meatballs): 206 Cal, 6 g Fat,
2 g Sat Fat, 0 g Trans Fat, 32 mg Chol, 740 mg Sod, 22 g Carb,
4 g Fib, 19 g Prot, 43 mg Calc. **POINTS** value: **4.**

Zap It Freeze the soup in single-serving microwavable
containers up to 2 months. When ready to serve,
microwave each container, partially covered, on High
until the soup is hot, 4 to 5 minutes.

Hearty Split-Pea Soup

❧

Hands-On Prep **15 MIN**
Cook **1 HR 30 MIN**
Serves **8**

1 Bring the peas and enough cold water to cover by
2 inches to a boil in a large saucepan. Remove the pan
from the heat. Let soak, covered, about 1 hour. Drain.

2 Heat the oil in a large nonstick saucepan over
medium-high heat. Add the carrots, onion, and celery;
cook, stirring occasionally, until softened, about
5 minutes. Add the drained peas, broth, water, ham,
and pepper; bring to a boil. Reduce the heat and
simmer, covered, stirring occasionally, until the peas
are tender, about 1 hour. Sprinkle with the cheese just
before serving.

PER SERVING (1 cup): 288 Cal, 6 g Fat, 2 g Sat Fat, 0 g Trans Fat,
11 mg Chol, 455 mg Sod, 39 g Carb, 15 g Fib, 21 g Prot, 93 mg Calc.
POINTS value: **5.**

1 (1-pound) package dried
   split peas, picked over,
   rinsed, and drained
4 teaspoons safflower oil
2 carrots, chopped
1 large onion, chopped
1 celery stalk, chopped
1 (32-ounce) carton
   reduced-sodium
   chicken broth
2 cups water
¼ pound lean ham, cut into
   matchstick-thin strips
¼ teaspoon freshly
   ground pepper
½ cup shredded reduced-fat
   cheddar cheese

Plan Ahead Make this soup over a weekend for an
instant meal later in the week; it can be refrigerated in
an airtight container up to 3 days. To reheat, thin the
soup with a little water, as needed (it will thicken as it
stands); place over medium heat and cook, stirring
occasionally, until warmed through. Top with the cheese
just before serving.

HEARTY SPLIT-PEA SOUP;
WHOLE-WHEAT ICEBOX
ROLLS, PAGE 180

Italian-Bread Soup

❧

Hands-On Prep **15 MIN**
Cook **1 HR 35 MIN**
Serves **8**

1 Heat the oil in a large nonstick saucepan over medium-high heat. Add the onions, bacon, and garlic; cook, stirring occasionally, until the onions are softened, about 5 minutes. Stir in the tomatoes with their juice, the carrots, and celery. Reduce the heat and simmer until the celery and carrots are partially softened, about 10 minutes. Stir in the kale, broth, beans, chopped sage, and pepper; bring to a boil. Reduce the heat and simmer, stirring frequently, until the kale is very tender and the soup has thickened, about 1 hour.

2 Place a layer of 4 bread slices in the bottom of another large saucepan or a Dutch oven. Add a few ladlefuls of the soup; then place the remaining bread on top. Pour in the remaining soup and bring to a boil. Reduce the heat and simmer until the bread is soft, about 10 minutes. Sprinkle with the slivered sage leaves and serve at once.

PER SERVING (generous 2 cups): 245 Cal, 5 g Fat, 1 g Sat Fat, 0 g Trans Fat, 2 mg Chol, 898 mg Sod, 38 g Carb, 8 g Fib, 13 g Prot, 145 mg Calc. *POINTS* value: **5.**

Try It Lacinato kale (sometimes called Tuscan kale or dinosaur kale) has tender, beautifully embossed dark blue-green leaves. It's sweeter and more delicate than regular kale, which has a pungent, peppery taste. You'll find lacinato kale in the produce section of larger supermarkets, or look for it at your local health food store or farmers' market.

4 teaspoons olive oil
2 onions, chopped
1 slice Canadian bacon, cut into matchstick-thin strips
2 garlic cloves, minced
1 (28-ounce) can whole plum tomatoes, coarsely chopped, with their juice
3 carrots, chopped
3 celery stalks, chopped
1 bunch lacinato or regular kale, trimmed and chopped
4 (14½-ounce) cans reduced-sodium chicken broth
2 (15-ounce) cans cannellini (white kidney) beans, rinsed and drained
2 tablespoons chopped fresh sage
¼ teaspoon freshly ground pepper
8 (1-ounce) slices stale Italian or French bread
2–3 tablespoons slivered fresh sage leaves

Louisiana Gumbo

Hands-On Prep **15 MIN**
Cook **45 MIN**
Serves **4**

1 Heat the oil in a large nonstick saucepan over medium-high heat. Add the bell pepper, scallions, celery, and garlic; cook, stirring occasionally, until softened, about 5 minutes. Add the tomatoes, broth, okra, bay leaf, thyme, and crushed red pepper; bring to a boil. Reduce the heat and simmer, covered, until the vegetables are softened, about 15 minutes.

2 Stir in the rice and cook until the rice is soft on the outside but still hard in the center, 15–20 minutes. Add the shrimp, chicken, and kielbasa; simmer, covered, just until the shrimp are opaque in the center, the chicken is cooked through, and the rice is tender, 5–10 minutes. Stir in the crabmeat and cook just until heated through, about 1 minute. Discard the bay leaf and serve at once.

PER SERVING (about 2¼ cups): 347 Cal, 8 g Fat, 1 g Sat Fat, 0 g Trans Fat, 176 mg Chol, 784 mg Sod, 37 g Carb, 5 g Fib, 33 g Prot, 186 mg Calc. *POINTS* value: **7.**

Good Idea Freeze chopped onions, bell pepper, celery, and other vegetables you use frequently in zip-close plastic bags. They'll last about 1 month, and having them on hand makes preparing soups like this one a cinch.

4 teaspoons safflower oil
1 green bell pepper, seeded and chopped
8 scallions, sliced
1 celery stalk, chopped
1 garlic clove, minced
1 (14½-ounce) can diced tomatoes
1 (14½-ounce) can reduced-sodium chicken broth
1 (10-ounce) box frozen okra, thawed
1 bay leaf
¾ teaspoon dried thyme
¼ teaspoon crushed red pepper
½ cup long-grain white rice
¾ pound medium shrimp, peeled and deveined
¼ pound skinless boneless chicken breast, cut into ½-inch pieces
2 ounces reduced-fat kielbasa, sliced
1 cup fresh or thawed frozen cooked crabmeat, picked over

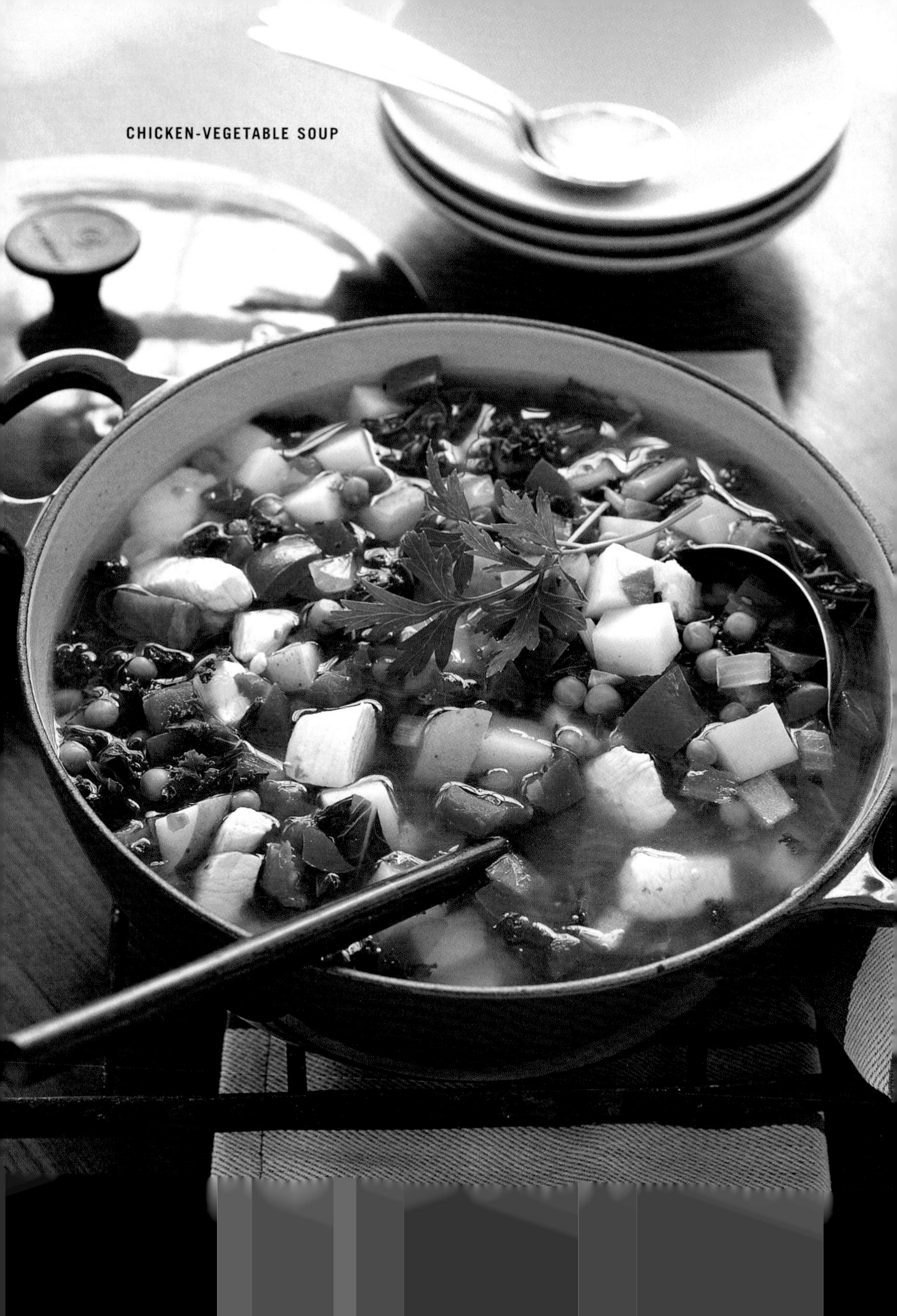

CHICKEN-VEGETABLE SOUP

Chicken-Vegetable Soup

Hands-On Prep **10 MIN**
Cook **30 MIN**
Serves **6**

1 Heat the oil in a large saucepan over medium heat. Add the onion, garlic, and thyme; cook, stirring frequently, until the onion has softened, about 2 minutes. Add the potatoes and kale; cook until the kale starts to wilt, 4–5 minutes. Stir in the broth and tomatoes; bring to a boil. Reduce the heat and simmer, covered, 15 minutes.

2 Stir in the chicken and peas; cook, covered, until the potatoes are tender and the chicken is cooked through, about 10 minutes. Serve with the pepper.

PER SERVING (1⅓ cups): 196 Cal, 3 g Fat, 1 g Sat Fat, 0 g Trans Fat, 31 mg Chol, 567 mg Sod, 25 g Carb, 5 g Fib, 18 g Prot, 73 mg Calc. **POINTS** value: **3.**

Good Idea If you'd like a vegetarian version of this soup, use an equal amount of vegetable broth and substitute a 15-ounce can of rinsed and drained chickpeas for the diced chicken.

2 teaspoons extra-virgin olive oil
1 onion, chopped
4 garlic cloves, minced
½ teaspoon dried thyme
¾ pound red potatoes, scrubbed and diced
4 cups chopped fresh kale
1 (32-ounce) carton reduced-sodium chicken broth
1 (14½-ounce) can diced tomatoes
¾ pound skinless boneless chicken breasts, diced
1 cup frozen peas
Freshly ground pepper, to taste

New England Fish Chowder

Hands-On Prep **15 MIN**
Cook **40 MIN**
Serves **4**

1 Bring the water, potatoes, onion, mushrooms, celery, and butter to a boil in a large saucepan. Reduce the heat and simmer, covered, until the potatoes are tender, about 20 minutes.

2 Place the flour in a medium bowl. Whisk in the milk and evaporated milk; stir into the potato mixture in the saucepan. Stir in the fish, broth, thyme, and pepper. Cook over medium heat, stirring frequently, just until the fish is opaque and the chowder has thickened slightly, about 15 minutes (do not boil). Garnish with the additional thyme and serve at once.

PER SERVING (1¼ cups): 215 Cal, 8 g Fat, 3 g Sat Fat, 0 g Trans Fat, 45 mg Chol, 136 mg Sod, 21 g Carb, 2 g Fib, 16 g Prot, 106 mg Calc. *POINTS* value: **5.**

Food Note Packed with fish and full of briny flavors, our chowder is a showcase for your market's freshest catch. Good choices include cod, sea bass, monkfish, orange roughy, red snapper, and tilefish.

1 cup water
2 all-purpose potatoes, peeled and chopped
1 onion, chopped
1 cup chopped fresh mushrooms
1 celery stalk, chopped
4 teaspoons butter
1 tablespoon all-purpose flour
1 cup fat-free milk
1 cup evaporated fat-free milk
½ pound firm-fleshed skinless whitefish fillets, cut into 1-inch pieces
1 (8-ounce) bottle clam juice
½ tablespoon chopped fresh thyme
Freshly ground pepper, to taste
2 teaspoons chopped fresh thyme, for garnish

Asian Shrimp and Noodle Soup

❧❧

Hands-On Prep **20 MIN**
Cook **20 MIN**
Serves **8**

1 Bring the broth to a boil in a large saucepan. Add the bok choy, snow peas, shrimp, soy sauce, and sesame oil; return to a boil. Reduce the heat and simmer just until the bok choy and snow peas are crisp-tender and the shrimp are opaque in the center, about 5 minutes.

2 Stir in the scallions, tofu, water chestnuts, cappellini, vinegar, and pepper. Cook until the capellini is barely tender and the soup is heated through, about 5 minutes. Serve at once.

PER SERVING (1¾ cups): 196 Cal, 6 g Fat, 1 g Sat Fat, 0 g Trans Fat, 28 mg Chol, 576 mg Sod, 21 g Carb, 4 g Fib, 16 g Prot, 139 mg Calc. *POINTS* value: *4.*

Try It Amber-colored and aromatic, Asian (dark) sesame oil is made from pressed toasted sesame seeds. It is best not to use this variety of oil for stir-frying or sautéing, as its flavor is intense and it burns quite easily. Instead, use sesame oil to enhance flavor, adding it during the final stages of cooking. Sesame oil will keep for several months if stored in the refrigerator.

- 2 (32-ounce) cartons reduced-sodium chicken broth
- 1 (½-pound) head bok choy, trimmed and sliced (4 cups)
- ¾ pound fresh snow peas, trimmed and cut into 1-inch pieces
- ¼ pound small shrimp, peeled and deveined
- 2 teaspoons reduced-sodium soy sauce
- 2 teaspoons Asian (dark) sesame oil
- 1 bunch scallions, trimmed and sliced
- ½ pound firm tofu, cut into ¼-inch slices and then into 1-inch squares
- 1 (8-ounce) can sliced water chestnuts, drained
- 4 ounces capellini
- 1 teaspoon rice vinegar
- ¼ teaspoon freshly ground pepper

Italian-Style Clam Chowder

❧

Hands-On Prep **20 MIN**
Cook **25 MIN**
Serves **4**

☑

1 Heat the oil in a large nonstick saucepan over medium-high heat. Add the fennel, onion, carrot, and celery; cook, stirring occasionally, until softened, about 5 minutes.

2 Add the hot water, tomatoes with their juice, the clam juice, potato, oregano, and pepper; bring to a boil. Reduce the heat and simmer, until the potatoes and vegetables are tender, about 15 minutes. Stir in the clams with their juice, the olives, capers, lemon zest, and lemon juice. Cook until heated through (do not boil) and serve at once.

PER SERVING (1½ cups): 156 Cal, 6 g Fat, 1 g Sat Fat, 0 g Trans Fat, 16 mg Chol, 520 mg Sod, 19 g Carb, 4 g Fib, 8 g Prot, 86 mg Calc. *POINTS* value: *3.*

Food Note If the soup becomes too thick while it cooks in step 2, add an additional 1 cup hot water, ½ cup at a time, before stirring in the clams and the remaining ingredients.

4 teaspoons olive oil
1½ cups chopped fresh fennel
1 onion, chopped
1 carrot, chopped
1 celery stalk, chopped
2½ cups hot water
1 cup canned stewed tomatoes, coarsely chopped, with their juice
1 (8-ounce) bottle clam juice
1 all-purpose potato, peeled and chopped
1 teaspoon dried oregano
¼ teaspoon freshly ground pepper
1 (6½-ounce) can minced clams with their juice
10 small brine-cured black olives, pitted and chopped
2 tablespoons capers, drained
½ teaspoon grated lemon zest
1 teaspoon fresh lemon juice

Classic Minestrone

❦

Hands-On Prep **25 MIN**
Cook **1 HR 40 MIN**
Serves **8**

1 Soak the beans according to package directions. Drain.

2 Combine the beans, broth, salt, and pepper in a large saucepan; bring just to a boil. Reduce the heat and simmer, covered, until the beans are barely tender, about 1 hour.

3 Meanwhile, heat the oil in a large nonstick skillet over medium-high heat. Add the onions, carrots, celery, and garlic; cook, stirring frequently, until softened, about 5 minutes.

4 Stir the vegetable mixture into the bean mixture; add the tomatoes and their juice, the cabbage, zucchini, parsley, and sage. Simmer, stirring occasionally, until the vegetables are tender, about 20 minutes. Stir in the tubetti and cook until barely tender, about 10 minutes. Remove the pan from the heat; cover and let stand until the tubetti is just tender, about 10 minutes. Serve, sprinkled with the cheese.

PER SERVING (1½ cups with 2 tablespoons cheese): 221 Cal, 5 g Fat, 1 g Sat Fat, 0 g Trans Fat, 2 mg Chol, 481 mg Sod, 34 g Carb, 8 g Fib, 12 g Prot, 143 mg Calc. *POINTS* value: *4.*

6 ounces dried cannellini (white kidney) beans, picked over, rinsed, and drained
2 (32-ounce) cartons reduced-sodium chicken broth
¼ teaspoon salt
¼ teaspoon freshly ground pepper
4 teaspoons olive oil
2 onions, chopped
2 carrots, chopped
2 celery stalks, chopped
1 garlic clove, minced
1 (28-ounce) can whole plum tomatoes, drained and chopped, with 1 cup of their juice reserved
1 (1-pound) green cabbage, shredded
3 zucchini, chopped
½ cup chopped parsley
2 teaspoons dried sage
3 ounces tubetti or other small pasta
¼ cup grated Parmesan cheese

Home-Style Lentil Soup

❧

Hands-On Prep **15 MIN**
Cook **50 MIN**
Serves **8**

1 Bring the broth, lentils, carrots, onions, celery, and bay leaf to a boil in a large saucepan. Reduce the heat and simmer, covered, stirring occasionally, until the lentils and vegetables are tender, about 30 minutes.

2 Stir in the tomatoes, tomato juice, vinegar, and pepper; gradually add the water until the desired thickness is reached. Cook, covered, stirring occasionally, until the flavors are blended, about 10 minutes. Discard the bay leaf.

PER SERVING (1¾ cups): 261 Cal, 2 g Fat, 0 g Sat Fat, 0 g Trans Fat, 0 mg Chol, 364 mg Sod, 44 g Carb, 15 g Fib, 19 g Prot, 72 mg Calc. *POINTS* value: *5.*

Plan Ahead Good news for busy cooks—hearty soups like this one taste even better if made in advance. Refrigerate this soup up to 5 days or freeze it up to 3 months. It will thicken slightly with time; just thin it with a little water when you reheat it on the stove top or in the microwave.

10 cups reduced-sodium beef broth
1 pound dried lentils, picked over, rinsed, and drained
4 carrots, chopped
2 large onions, peeled and chopped
1 celery stalk, chopped
1 bay leaf
3 canned whole plum tomatoes, drained and chopped
1 cup tomato juice
1 tablespoon apple-cider vinegar
¼ teaspoon freshly ground pepper
1–2 cups hot water

Spinach Egg-Drop Soup

෴

☑

1 Bring the broth, ginger, and soy sauce to a boil in a large saucepan. Reduce the heat and simmer until the flavors are blended, about 10 minutes.

2 Slowly add the eggs and cook, whisking constantly to form strands, about 1 minute. Remove the pan from the heat; discard the ginger. Add the spinach, scallions, and cilantro; cook, stirring constantly, just until the spinach wilts. Serve at once.

PER SERVING (1¼ cups): 82 Cal, 4 g Fat, 1 g Sat Fat, 0 g Trans Fat, 159 mg Chol, 839 mg Sod, 4 g Carb, 1 g Fib, 8 g Prot, 32 mg Calc. ***POINTS*** value: **2.**

1 (32-ounce) carton reduced-sodium chicken broth
4 quarter-size slices fresh ginger
1 tablespoon reduced-sodium soy sauce
3 large eggs, lightly beaten
2 cups baby spinach leaves
2 scallions, chopped
2 tablespoons chopped fresh cilantro

Good Idea To make a more substantial soup, add 1 cup shredded cooked chicken breast with the eggs in step 2. The per-serving ***POINTS*** value will increase by ***1.***

Creamy Asparagus Soup

Hands-On Prep **10 MIN**
Cook **40 MIN**
Serves **6**

1 Heat the oil in a large saucepan over medium heat. Add the onion and cook, stirring occasionally, until softened, about 6 minutes. Add the potato and thyme; cook, stirring frequently, until well coated, about 1 minute. Stir in the broth and asparagus; bring to a boil. Reduce the heat and simmer until the vegetables are very tender, about 20 minutes. Stir in the evaporated milk, salt, and pepper; cook until heated through, about 5 minutes.

2 Let the mixture cool about 5 minutes. Pour into a blender and puree, in batches if necessary. Divide the soup among 6 bowls and swirl 1 tablespoon of sour cream into each serving.

PER SERVING (1 cup): 116 Cal, 2 g Fat, 0 g Sat Fat, 0 g Trans Fat, 3 mg Chol, 595 mg Sod, 18 g Carb, 2 g Fib, 8 g Prot, 154 mg Calc. ***POINTS*** value: **2.**

Good Idea When choosing asparagus, look for firm, green spears with tight, crisp tips. The spears should snap easily when bent. You can also try this easy trick: Give a bunch a squeeze—if it squeaks, it's fresh!

2 teaspoons extra-virgin olive oil
1 onion, chopped
1 large baking potato, peeled and cut into 1-inch cubes
½ teaspoon dried thyme
1 (32-ounce) carton reduced-sodium chicken broth
1 pound fresh asparagus, trimmed and cut into 1-inch pieces
1 cup evaporated fat-free milk
¼ teaspoon salt
¼ teaspoon freshly ground pepper
6 tablespoons fat-free sour cream

French Onion Soup

❧

Hands-On Prep **15 MIN**
Cook **40 MIN**
Serves **4**

1 Heat the oil in a large nonstick skillet over medium-high heat. Add the onions and cook, stirring frequently, until golden, about 15 minutes.

2 Meanwhile, preheat the oven to 450°F. Place 4 ovenproof soup bowls on a baking sheet.

3 Bring the broth to a simmer in a large saucepan. Add the onions, Worcestershire sauce, and pepper. Reduce the heat and simmer, stirring occasionally, until the onions are tender, about 15 minutes. Ladle the soup into the bowls; top each serving with 1 slice of bread and ¼ cup of the cheese. Bake until the cheese melts, about 5 minutes, and serve at once.

4 teaspoons olive oil
2 pounds onions, thinly sliced
1 (32-ounce) carton reduced-sodium beef broth
1½ teaspoons Worcestershire sauce
¼ teaspoon freshly ground pepper
4 (1-ounce) slices French bread, toasted
1 cup shredded reduced-fat Swiss cheese

PER SERVING (1 cup): 299 Cal, 11 g Fat, 4 g Sat Fat, 0 g Trans Fat, 9 mg Chol, 689 mg Sod, 34 g Carb, 5 g Fib, 18 g Prot, 410 mg Calc. *POINTS* value: *6.*

Plan Ahead To enjoy this soup another time, prepare the recipe as directed except double the oil and onions and cook in a Dutch oven in step 1. Then double the broth, Worcestershire sauce, and pepper in step 3. Before ladling the soup into the bowls, freeze the extra portion in an airtight container up to 1 month. To serve, thaw in the refrigerator overnight and reheat on the stove top. Then all you have to do at the last minute is toast the bread and shred the cheese.

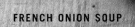
FRENCH ONION SOUP

Winter Squash Soup with Sage

Hands-On Prep **15 MIN**
Cook **35 MIN**
Serves **4**

1 Heat the oil in a large nonstick saucepan over medium-high heat. Add the onion and cook, stirring frequently, until softened, about 5 minutes. Add the squash, broth, and 2 tablespoons of the sage; bring to a boil. Reduce the heat and simmer, adding the water ½ cup at a time, until the squash is very soft, about 20 minutes. Remove the pan from the heat and let cool 30 minutes.

2 Strain the squash mixture through a sieve into a bowl; reserve the cooking liquid. Transfer the squash mixture to a food processor; pulse, in batches if necessary, until very smooth. Add 1–1½ cups of the reserved cooking liquid, ½ cup at a time, until the soup has a fluid but creamy consistency.

3 Return the soup to the saucepan and cook over medium-high heat, stirring frequently, just until heated through, about 5 minutes. Top each serving with 1 tablespoon of the sour cream and garnish with the remaining 2 tablespoons of sage.

2 teaspoons extra-virgin olive oil
1 onion, chopped
1 (2-pound) butternut squash, peeled, seeded, and coarsely chopped
1 (32-ounce) carton reduced-sodium chicken broth
4 tablespoons chopped fresh sage
1–1½ cups water
4 tablespoons fat-free sour cream

PER SERVING (1 cup): 184 Cal, 4 g Fat, 1 g Sat Fat, 0 g Trans Fat, 0 mg Chol, 489 mg Sod, 33 g Carb, 7 g Fib, 8 g Prot, 136 mg Calc. *POINTS* value: *3.*

Good Idea If you have any cooking liquid left over from step 2, save it for flavoring stews and other soups. It will last in an airtight container up to 3 days in the refrigerator or 2 months in the freezer.

French Potato-Leek Soup

Hands-On Prep **25 MIN**
Cook **40 MIN**
Serves **8**

☑

1 Bring the broth, potatoes, leeks, and pepper to a boil in a large saucepan. Reduce the heat and simmer, covered, until the vegetables are very soft, about 30 minutes. Uncover and let the mixture cool about 5 minutes.

2 In a food processor, puree, in batches if necessary, at least 2 cups or all of the potatoes and leeks (depending on the texture you prefer) with 1–2 cups of the cooking liquid. Stir the puree into the remaining soup and reheat. Serve at once or refrigerate until cold and serve chilled, garnished with the scallions.

PER SERVING (1½ cups): 153 Cal, 1 g Fat, 0 g Sat Fat, 0 g Trans Fat, 0 mg Chol, 477 mg Sod, 28 g Carb, 3 g Fib, 7 g Prot, 44 mg Calc. **POINTS** value: **3.**

- 2 (32-ounce) cartons reduced-sodium chicken broth
- 2½ pounds all-purpose potatoes, peeled and chopped
- 3 leeks, cleaned and thinly sliced (white and light green parts only)
- ¼ teaspoon freshly ground pepper
- 2 tablespoons minced scallions, for garnish

How We Did It We find that the best way to clean leeks is to trim the roots, leaving the root end intact to hold the layers together. Then slice the leeks lengthwise, fan open the layers, and swish in a large bowl of cool water. Let the leeks stand a few minutes to allow the grit to fall to the bottom of the bowl; then lift them out.

Chilled Borscht with Sour Cream

❧

Hands-On Prep **25 MIN**
Cook **35 MIN**
Serves **4**

1 Bring the beets, broth, water, red onion, cabbage, and brown sugar to a boil in a large saucepan. Reduce the heat and simmer, covered, until the cabbage is tender, about 20 minutes. Stir in 2 tablespoons of the dill and simmer until the flavors are blended, about 5 minutes.

2 Remove the pan from the heat. Stir in the lemon juice, salt, and pepper. Transfer to an airtight container and refrigerate until chilled, at least 2 hours or up to 3 days. When ready to serve, top each serving with 1 tablespoon of the sour cream and ½ tablespoon of the remaining dill.

PER SERVING (1 cup): 68 Cal, 1 g Fat, 0 g Sat Fat, 0 g Trans Fat, 0 mg Chol, 294 mg Sod, 13 g Carb, 2 g Fib, 4 g Prot, 62 mg Calc. **POINTS** value: *1.*

Good Idea Since peeling fresh beets can stain your skin, wearing kitchen gloves is a wise move. If you don't have a pair of gloves handy and your hands become stained, rub them with some fresh lemon juice and then rinse under cold running water.

¾ **pound fresh beets, trimmed, peeled, and shredded (2 cups)**

1 **(14½-ounce) can reduced-sodium beef broth**

1½ **cups water**

½ **red onion, finely chopped**

½ **cup finely shredded red cabbage**

½ **teaspoon packed brown sugar**

4 **tablespoons chopped fresh dill**

2 **tablespoons fresh lemon juice**

¼ **teaspoon salt**

¼ **teaspoon freshly ground pepper**

4 **tablespoons fat-free sour cream**

Cucumber-Yogurt Soup

❧

Hands-On Prep **15 MIN**
Cook **NONE**
Serves **4**

1 Puree, in batches if necessary, the coarsely chopped cucumbers, yogurt, onion, jalapeño, water, lemon juice, salt, and pepper in a blender. Transfer to a large bowl and refrigerate until chilled, at least 2 hours or overnight.

2 When ready to serve, stir in the tomatoes, the finely chopped cucumber, and the cilantro until blended. Serve at once.

PER SERVING (1 generous cup): 82 Cal, 0 g Fat, 0 g Sat Fat, 0 g Trans Fat, 3 mg Chol, 510 mg Sod, 17 g Carb, 2 g Fib, 6 g Prot, 176 mg Calc. **POINTS** value: **1.**

Good Idea If you are planning to chill this soup overnight, whisk until blended before adding the remaining ingredients in step 2.

- 2 **medium cucumbers, peeled, seeded, and coarsely chopped**
- 2 **cups plain fat-free yogurt**
- 1 **small onion, chopped**
- 1 **jalapeño pepper, halved and seeded (wear gloves to prevent irritation)**
- ⅓ **cup water**
- 2 **tablespoons fresh lemon juice**
- ¾ **teaspoon salt**
- ¼ **teaspoon freshly ground pepper**
- 1 **cup cherry tomatoes, quartered**
- 1 **small cucumber, peeled, seeded, and finely chopped**
- 2 **tablespoons fresh chopped cilantro**

Pasta and Pizza Favorites

CHAPTER 5

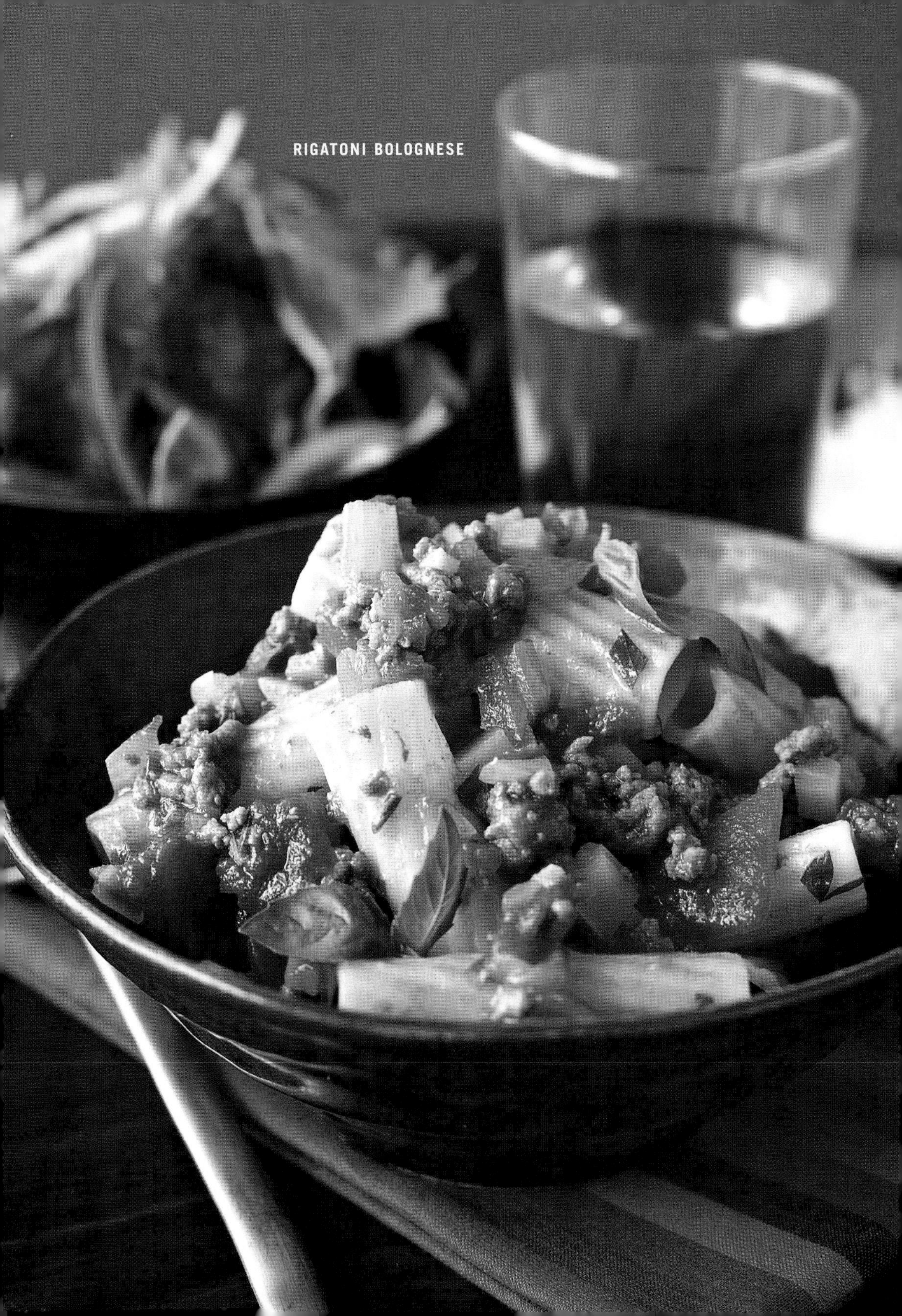

RIGATONI BOLOGNESE

Rigatoni Bolognese

Hands-On Prep **15 MIN**
Cook **1 HR 5 MIN**
Serves **4**

1 To make the sauce, heat the oil in a large nonstick saucepan over medium-high heat. Add the onion and cook, stirring frequently, until softened, about 5 minutes. Add the celery, carrot, and garlic; cook, stirring frequently, until the vegetables are softened, about 5 minutes. Add the beef and cook until browned, about 5 minutes, breaking it apart with a wooden spoon. Stir in the tomatoes, parsley, wine, rosemary, bay leaf, salt, and pepper. Cook, stirring occasionally, until bubbly, about 5 minutes. Reduce the heat and simmer, stirring occasionally, until thickened, about 45 minutes. Discard the rosemary and bay leaf.

2 Meanwhile, cook the rigatoni according to package directions, omitting the salt if desired. Drain and transfer to a large bowl; add the sauce and toss. Sprinkle with the cheese and basil just before serving.

PER SERVING (1½ cups with 1 tablespoon cheese): 315 Cal, 7 g Fat, 3 g Sat Fat, 0 g Trans Fat, 35 mg Chol, 543 mg Sod, 43 g Carb, 6 g Fib, 21 g Prot, 136 mg Calc. *POINTS* value: *6.*

Plan Ahead Make a double, triple, or quadruple batch of sauce and freeze it up to 3 months. In a pinch, it can go straight from freezer to stove top or microwave, but if you have the time, a preferable method is to thaw it overnight in the refrigerator.

- 2 teaspoons olive oil
- 1 onion, finely chopped
- 1 celery stalk, finely chopped
- 1 carrot, finely chopped
- 1 garlic clove, minced
- ½ pound ground lean beef (5% fat or less) or ground skinless turkey breast
- 1 (28-ounce) can diced tomatoes
- ¼ cup finely chopped flat-leaf parsley
- ¼ cup dry red wine or reduced-sodium beef broth
- 1 fresh rosemary sprig
- 1 bay leaf
- ¼ teaspoon salt
- Freshly ground pepper, to taste
- 2 cups rigatoni
- ¼ cup grated Parmesan cheese
- Fresh basil leaves

Mama's Baked Ziti with Meatballs

Hands-On Prep **30 MIN**
Cook **1 HR 5 MIN**
Serves **8**

1 Heat the oil in a large nonstick saucepan over medium-high heat. Add the onion and garlic; cook, stirring frequently, until softened, about 5 minutes. Stir in the drained tomatoes. Reduce the heat and cook, stirring occasionally, until bubbly, about 5 minutes.

2 In a large bowl, combine the beef, pork, Parmesan cheese, ½ cup of the parsley, the bread crumbs, egg whites, basil, oregano, thyme, salt, and pepper. Form into 40 walnut-size meatballs and drop gently into the bubbling sauce. Simmer, without stirring, until the meatballs are firm, about 15 minutes. Stir in the remaining ½ cup of parsley and cook, stirring occasionally and adding the reserved tomato juice ¼ cup at a time, until the meatballs are tender and the sauce has thickened, about 20 minutes.

3 Preheat the oven to 400°F. Spray a 9 x 13-inch baking dish with nonstick spray.

4 Meanwhile, cook the ziti according to package directions, omitting the salt if desired. Drain and toss in a large bowl with the sauce and meatballs. Transfer the mixture to the baking dish; sprinkle with the mozzarella cheese. Cover with foil and bake until heated through, 15–20 minutes. Uncover; bake until bubbly and golden, 5–10 minutes.

PER SERVING (1 cup ziti and sauce with 5 meatballs): 302 Cal, 6 g Fat, 2 g Sat Fat, 0 g Trans Fat, 29 mg Chol, 525 mg Sod, 42 g Carb, 3 g Fib, 19 g Prot, 105 mg Calc. **POINTS** value: **6.**

1 tablespoon olive oil
1 onion, finely chopped
1 garlic clove, minced
1 (28-ounce) can diced tomatoes, drained, with their juice reserved
½ **pound ground lean beef (5% fat or less)**
¼ **pound ground lean pork**
¼ **cup grated Parmesan cheese**
1 cup chopped flat-leaf parsley
½ cup plain dried bread crumbs
2 egg whites or ¼ cup fat-free egg substitute
1 tablespoon chopped fresh basil, or 1 teaspoon dried
1 teaspoon chopped fresh oregano or marjoram, or ½ teaspoon dried
1 teaspoon chopped fresh thyme, or ¼ teaspoon dried
¼ teaspoon salt
Freshly ground pepper, to taste
4 cups ziti
¼ cup shredded part-skim mozzarella cheese

Spaghetti alla Carbonara

Hands-On Prep **10 MIN**
Cook **20 MIN**
Serves **4**

1 Cook the spaghetti according to package
directions, omitting the salt if desired.

2 Meanwhile, melt the butter in a large nonstick
skillet over medium-high heat. Add the bacon,
shallot, and garlic; cook, stirring frequently, until the
bacon and shallot are browned and the garlic cloves
are golden, about 5 minutes. Discard the garlic.

3 Drain the spaghetti and immediately add it to the
skillet; set the skillet over low heat. Add the egg
substitute and cheese; toss to coat. Cook, stirring
constantly, just until the egg is cooked through, about
2 minutes. Sprinkle with the parsley and pepper and
serve at once.

6 ounces spaghetti
4 teaspoons butter
4 (1-ounce) slices
Canadian bacon, trimmed
and cut into matchstick-
thin strips
1 shallot, finely chopped
2 garlic cloves, bruised
⅔ cup fat-free egg
substitute
¼ cup grated Parmesan
cheese
1 tablespoon finely
chopped flat-leaf parsley
¼ teaspoon freshly
ground pepper

PER SERVING (¾ cup): 288 Cal, 8 g Fat, 4 g Sat Fat, 0 g Trans Fat,
29 mg Chol, 475 mg Sod, 36 g Carb, 2 g Fib, 16 g Prot, 78 mg Calc.
POINTS value: **6.**

Good Idea If the spaghetti is not quite done
by the time you have completed step 2, remove the
skillet from the heat and set it aside until you're
ready to add the drained pasta.

Capellini with Seafood and Herbs

❧❧

Hands-On Prep **15 MIN**
Cook **20 MIN**
Serves **4**

1 Combine the clams, mussels, broth, and garlic in a large saucepan. Cook, covered, over medium heat until the shells open, about 8 minutes. Discard any shells that do not open. Set the clams and mussels aside with their cooking liquid.

2 Heat the oil in a large nonstick skillet over medium-high heat. Add the scallops, shrimp, and the chopped parsley, thyme, and oregano; cook, stirring constantly, just until the shrimp and scallops are opaque in the center, about 5 minutes. Remove the skillet from the heat; stir in the clam and mussel mixture.

3 Meanwhile, cook the capellini according to package directions, omitting the salt if desired. Drain and transfer to a large bowl; top with the seafood mixture, sprinkle with the pepper, and toss to combine. Garnish with the herb sprigs and serve at once.

PER SERVING (1 cup): 321 Cal, 5 g Fat, 1 g Sat Fat, 0 g Trans Fat, 81 mg Chol, 303 mg Sod, 39 g Carb, 2 g Fib, 29 g Prot, 110 mg Calc. *POINTS* value: **6.**

12 cherrystone clams, scrubbed
12 mussels, scrubbed and debearded
¼ cup reduced-sodium vegetable broth
2 garlic cloves, minced
2 teaspoons extra-virgin olive oil
½ pound bay scallops
¼ pound medium shrimp, peeled and deveined
2 tablespoons chopped fresh parsley
1 tablespoon chopped fresh thyme
1 tablespoon chopped fresh oregano
6 ounces capellini
¼ teaspoon freshly ground pepper
Fresh parsley, thyme, and/or oregano sprigs

How We Did It To prep the clams and mussels, scrub them well with a vegetable brush under cold running water. Place the clams and mussels in a large pot of cold water; let them soak 5 minutes to release any residual grit, and drain. Repeat with several changes of water, until no sand falls to the bottom of the pot.

CAPELLINI WITH
SEAFOOD AND HERBS

Pasta with Red Clam Sauce

⚜

Hands-On Prep **20 MIN**
Cook **25 MIN**
Serves **4**

1 Combine the clams, wine, thyme, oregano, garlic, and crushed red pepper in a large saucepan. Cover and cook over medium heat until the clams open, about 5 minutes. Transfer the clams to a bowl with a slotted spoon; reserve the cooking liquid, including the garlic and herbs. Discard any clams that do not open. When the clams are cool enough to handle, remove the meat and discard the shells. Coarsely chop the clams and set aside.

2 Cook the spaghetti according to package directions, omitting the salt if desired. Drain and transfer a large bowl; keep warm.

3 Meanwhile, heat the oil in a medium nonstick skillet over medium heat. Add the tomatoes, basil, 2 tablespoons of the parsley, and the anchovy paste; cook, stirring occasionally, about 5 minutes. Stir in the reserved cooking liquid; reduce the heat and simmer until thickened, about 5 minutes. Stir in the reserved clams and cook just until heated through. Add the sauce to the spaghetti and toss to coat. Sprinkle with the remaining 1 tablespoon of parsley. Serve at once.

12 cherrystone clams, scrubbed
¼ cup dry white wine or reduced-sodium vegetable broth
1 teaspoon dried thyme
1 teaspoon dried oregano
3 large garlic cloves, minced
¼ teaspoon crushed red pepper
6 ounces spaghetti
4 teaspoons olive oil
8 plum tomatoes, chopped
2 tablespoons chopped fresh basil
3 tablespoons finely chopped flat-leaf parsley
½ teaspoon anchovy paste

PER SERVING (1 cup): 270 Cal, 6 g Fat, 1 g Sat Fat, 0 g Trans Fat, 14 mg Chol, 71 mg Sod, 41 g Carb, 3 g Fib, 12 g Prot, 50 mg Calc. *POINTS* value: **5.**

Easy Vegetable Lasagna

❧❧

Hands-On Prep **20 MIN**
Cook **1 HR 10 MIN**
Serves **4**

1 Preheat the oven to 400°F. Spray 2 large baking sheets and an 8-inch-square baking dish with nonstick spray. Arrange the eggplant and zucchini slices on the baking sheets. Spray with nonstick spray, sprinkle with the salt and ground pepper, and bake until tender, about 15 minutes. Set aside.

2 Meanwhile, heat the oil in a large nonstick skillet over medium-high heat. Add the garlic and cook, stirring, until fragrant. Add the tomatoes, mushrooms, bell pepper, basil, and more ground pepper. Reduce the heat and cook until the sauce is bubbly but not yet thickened, about 10 minutes.

3 Spread ½ cup of the sauce in the baking dish. Cover with 1 or 2 lasagna noodles (depending on their size); top with one quarter of the eggplant and zucchini slices, then with another ½ cup of the sauce. Sprinkle with 1 tablespoon of the cheese. Repeat to make 4 more layers, ending with a layer of noodles topped with sauce. If any sauce remains, pour it on the top and around the edges of the lasagna.

4 Cover the dish with foil and bake until bubbly, about 35 minutes. Uncover and bake until all the sauce has been absorbed, 10–15 minutes. Let stand about 5 minutes; then cut into quarters.

1 (1-pound) eggplant, peeled and cut into ¼-inch slices
1 zucchini, cut into ¼-inch slices
¼ teaspoon salt
Freshly ground pepper, to taste
1 tablespoon olive oil
1 garlic clove, minced
1 (28-ounce) can whole tomatoes, chopped, with their juice
1 (10-ounce) package fresh mushrooms, sliced
1 large red bell pepper, seeded and finely chopped
½ cup chopped fresh basil
5 (6½ x 7-inch) sheets or 10 (3½ x 6½-inch) sheets no-boil lasagna noodles
4 tablespoons grated Parmesan cheese

PER SERVING (¼th of lasagna): 365 Cal, 8 g Fat, 2 g Sat Fat, 0 g Trans Fat, 5 mg Chol, 599 mg Sod, 62 g Carb, 9 g Fib, 15 g Prot, 182 mg Calc. **POINTS** value: **7.**

THAI NOODLES WITH TOFU

Thai Noodles with Tofu

Hands-On Prep **15 MIN**
Cook **25 MIN**
Serves **6**

1 Place the tofu between 2 flat plates. Weight the top plate with a heavy can until the tofu bulges at the sides but does not split. Let stand about 30 minutes; then pour off the water that has accumulated on the bottom of the plate. Cut the tofu into ½-inch cubes.

2 Meanwhile, bring a large pot of water to a boil. Add the noodles and cook until tender, 6–8 minutes. Drain the noodles and rinse under cold running water; drain again and set aside.

3 Combine the ketchup, fish sauce, brown sugar, and chili-garlic paste in a small bowl; set aside. Heat 2 teaspoons of the oil in a large nonstick skillet over medium-high heat. Add the eggs and cook, stirring occasionally, just until set, about 2 minutes. Transfer the eggs to a bowl.

4 Heat the remaining 2 teaspoons of oil in the skillet over medium-high heat. Add the garlic and cook, stirring constantly, just until fragrant, about 30 seconds. Add the tofu and cook, stirring occasionally, until hot, about 3 minutes. Add the scallions and the cooked eggs; cook, stirring, about 1 minute. Add the noodles and the ketchup mixture; cook, tossing, just until heated through, about 3 minutes. Transfer to a platter. Sprinkle with the peanuts and serve at once with the bean sprouts and lime wedges.

¾ **pound reduced-fat firm tofu**
½ **pound rice stick noodles**
6 **tablespoons ketchup**
3 **tablespoons Thai fish sauce (nam pla)**
2 **tablespoons packed dark brown sugar**
1 **teaspoon chili-garlic paste**
4 **teaspoons peanut oil**
2 **large eggs, lightly beaten**
3 **garlic cloves, minced**
4 **scallions, cut into ½-inch pieces**
2 **tablespoons chopped unsalted peanuts**
2 **cups bean sprouts**
Lime wedges

PER SERVING (1 cup): 313 Cal, 9 g Fat, 1 g Sat Fat, 0 g Trans Fat, 71 mg Chol, 993 mg Sod, 47 g Carb, 3 g Fib, 12 g Prot, 66 mg Calc. *POINTS* value: **6**.

Fusilli with Creamy Gorgonzola Sauce

Hands-On Prep **10 MIN**
Cook **20 MIN**
Serves **4**

1 Cook the fusilli according to package directions, omitting the salt if desired. Drain and transfer to a large bowl.

2 Meanwhile, combine the ricotta cheese, broth, and lemon zest in a medium bowl; mix until smooth. Spoon over the fusilli; then add the walnuts (if using), Gorgonzola cheese, and parsley; toss to coat. Serve at once or at room temperature.

PER SERVING without walnuts (1 cup): 196 Cal, 3 g Fat, 2 g Sat Fat, 0 g Trans Fat, 11 mg Chol, 168 mg Sod, 32 g Carb, 2 g Fib, 9 g Prot, 98 mg Calc. **POINTS** value: **4.**

2 cups fusilli
½ cup fat-free ricotta cheese
¼ cup reduced-sodium chicken broth
1 teaspoon grated lemon zest
¼ cup coarsely chopped walnuts (optional)
¼ cup crumbled Gorgonzola cheese
2 tablespoons chopped flat-leaf parsley

Food Note We've chosen fusilli for this speedy dish because its twists capture and hold bits of cheese and nuts, but any ridged, chunky pasta— such as cavatappi or rigatoni—will do nicely. If you wish to include the optional nuts, the per-serving **POINTS** value will increase by **1.**

Pasta with Tomatoes, Goat Cheese, and Basil

❧

Hands-On Prep **15 MIN**
Cook **20 MIN**
Serves **4**

1 Cook the rotelle according to package directions, omitting the salt if desired. Drain and transfer to a large bowl.

2 Meanwhile, heat the oil in a large nonstick skillet over medium-high heat. Add the garlic clove and cook, stirring constantly, just until fragrant, about 30 seconds. Discard the garlic. Add the tomatoes, salt, and pepper; cook, stirring occasionally, until the tomatoes have begun to release some of their juice, about 3 minutes.

3 Pour the tomato mixture over the rotelle; top with the cheese and basil; toss to coat. Serve at once or at room temperature.

2 cups rotelle
4 teaspoons extra-virgin olive oil
1 garlic clove, bruised
6 plum tomatoes, chopped
¼ teaspoon salt
Freshly ground pepper, to taste
2 ounces herbed or plain goat cheese, crumbled
½ cup chopped fresh basil

PER SERVING (1½ cups): 235 Cal, 8 g Fat, 3 g Sat Fat, 0 g Trans Fat, 13 mg Chol, 202 mg Sod, 33 g Carb, 2 g Fib, 8 g Prot, 91 mg Calc. **POINTS** value: **5.**

Food Note For a stronger garlic flavor, finely chop the clove and leave it in the oil after cooking it in step 2.

Penne with Vodka and Tomato

Hands-On Prep **10 MIN**
Cook **25 MIN**
Serves **4**

1 Cook the penne according to package directions, omitting the salt if desired. Drain and transfer to a large bowl.

2 Meanwhile, melt the butter in a medium nonstick skillet over medium-high heat. Add the shallot and tomato; cook, stirring frequently, until softened, about 5 minutes. Stir in the broth, tomato paste, and crushed red pepper; bring to a boil. Reduce the heat; then add the cream and vodka. Cook, stirring constantly, just until heated through (do not boil). Pour the sauce over the penne and toss to coat. Sprinkle with the cheese and parsley. Serve at once.

PER SERVING (³⁄₄ cup): 247 Cal, 10 g Fat, 8 g Sat Fat, 0 g Trans Fat, 38 mg Chol, 98 mg Sod, 32 g Carb, 2 g Fib, 7 g Prot, 58 mg Calc.
POINTS value: **5.**

2 cups penne
1 tablespoon unsalted
   butter
1 shallot, finely chopped
1 plum tomato, chopped
¼ cup reduced-sodium
   vegetable broth
1 tablespoon tomato paste
¼ teaspoon crushed
   red pepper
¼ cup heavy cream
2 tablespoons vodka or
   reduced-sodium
   vegetable broth
2 tablespoons grated
   Asiago cheese
2 tablespoons minced
   flat-leaf parsley

Good Idea If you like, serve this indulgent pasta with warm crusty Italian bread to soak up every drop of the creamy sauce. A 1-ounce piece with each serving will increase the ***POINTS*** value by **2.**

Rigatoni with Spinach, Ricotta, and Raisins

❧❧❧

Hands-On Prep **10 MIN**
Cook **20 MIN**
Serves **4**

1 Cook the rigatoni according to package directions, omitting the salt if desired. Drain and transfer to a large bowl.

2 Meanwhile, heat the oil in a medium nonstick skillet over medium heat. Add the onion and cook, stirring frequently, until softened, about 8 minutes. Stir in the spinach, raisins, and salt. Reduce the heat and cook, stirring occasionally, until heated through, about 3 minutes.

3 Combine the rigatoni, the spinach mixture, and ricotta and Parmesan cheeses; toss to coat. Sprinkle with the pepper and serve at once.

PER SERVING (1¼ cups): 298 Cal, 7 g Fat, 3 g Sat Fat, 0 g Trans Fat, 10 mg Chol, 325 mg Sod, 47 g Carb, 4 g Fib, 12 g Prot, 217 mg Calc. *POINTS* value: **6.**

Good Idea Instead of the spinach, try other greens—like broccolini, broccoli, broccoli rabe, or Swiss chard—in this recipe. Chop and steam until tender but still bright green, about 10 minutes; drain in a colander under cold running water to stop the cooking. Then proceed with the recipe as directed in step 3.

- 2 cups rigatoni
- 1 tablespoon extra-virgin olive oil
- 1 onion, chopped
- 1 (10-ounce) box frozen chopped spinach, thawed and squeezed dry
- ¼ cup raisins
- ¼ teaspoon salt
- ¼ cup part-skim ricotta cheese
- ¼ cup grated Parmesan cheese
- ¼ teaspoon freshly ground pepper

Ham and Bell Pepper Calzones

～❦～

Hands-On Prep **10 MIN**
Cook **30 MIN**
Serves **4**

1 Preheat the oven to 400°F. Spray a baking sheet with nonstick spray.

2 Heat the oil in a large nonstick skillet over medium-high heat. Add the onion, bell peppers, garlic, and oregano; cook, stirring occasionally, until softened, 5–7 minutes. Add the ham and cook, stirring occasionally, until lightly browned, about 3 minutes. Set the skillet aside and let the pepper and ham mixture cool.

3 Sprinkle a work surface lightly with flour. Turn the pizza dough onto the surface; cut in half. With a lightly floured rolling pin, roll each piece into a 10-inch circle. Spread half the ham mixture over half of one circle and spread the other half over half of the other circle, leaving a 1-inch border. Top the mixture on each pizza with the cheese. Fold the dough over the filling, crimping the edges to seal.

4 Transfer the calzones to the baking sheet. Bake until golden brown, about 20 minutes. Let cool 5 minutes. Cut each calzone in half.

2 teaspoons olive oil
1 onion, sliced
1 green bell pepper, seeded and cut into thin strips
1 red bell pepper, seeded and cut into thin strips
2 garlic cloves, minced
1 teaspoon dried oregano
¼ pound thin-sliced lean deli ham, cut crosswise into thin strips
1 pound refrigerated or thawed frozen pizza dough
1 cup shredded fat-free mozzarella cheese

PER SERVING (½ calzone): 384 Cal, 5 g Fat, 1 g Sat Fat, 0 g Trans Fat, 16 mg Chol, 985 mg Sod, 62 g Carb, 4 g Fib, 22 g Prot, 542 mg Calc. ***POINTS*** value: **7.**

Food Note When making calzones, don't use the refrigerated ready-made dough that comes in a pop-open tube; it won't be enough for this recipe.

HAM AND BELL PEPPER
CALZONES

Orecchiette with Broccoli Rabe

Hands-On Prep **10 MIN**
Cook **20 MIN**
Serves **4**

1 Bring a large pot of water to a boil. Add the broccoli rabe and 1 teaspoon of the salt; cook until bright green, about 2 minutes. Transfer with a slotted spoon to a colander and rinse under cold running water; squeeze out the excess water and set aside.

2 Return the water to a boil. Add the orecchiette and cook according to package directions, omitting the salt if desired. Drain and transfer to a large bowl.

3 Meanwhile, heat the oil in a large nonstick skillet over medium-high heat. Add the garlic and crushed red pepper; cook, stirring constantly, just until the garlic begins to brown, about 1 minute. Add the broth and bring to a boil. Add the broccoli rabe and cook, stirring frequently, until heated through, about 2 minutes.

4 Combine the orecchiette, broccoli rabe mixture, cheese, and the remaining ¼ teaspoon of salt; toss to coat. Serve at once or at room temperature.

1 pound broccoli rabe, trimmed and chopped
1¼ teaspoons salt
1⅓ cups orecchiette
5 teaspoons extra-virgin olive oil
6 garlic cloves, thinly sliced
¼ teaspoon crushed red pepper
¾ cup reduced-sodium chicken broth
¼ cup grated Parmesan cheese

PER SERVING (1¼ cups): 219 Cal, 8 g Fat, 2 g Sat Fat, 0 g Trans Fat, 4 mg Chol, 460 mg Sod, 26 g Carb, 3 g Fib, 10 g Prot, 233 mg Calc. *POINTS* value: *4.*

Try It *Orecchiette* ("little ears") is the perfect pasta for this dish, as its shape catches and holds the flavorful bits of broccoli rabe. If it's not available, small shells make a good substitute.

Southwest Pizza

~❧~

Hands-On Prep **10 MIN**
Cook **10 MIN**
Serves **4**

1 Place an oven rack on the bottom rung of the oven. Preheat the oven to 500°F.

2 Sprinkle a work surface lightly with flour. Turn the dough onto the surface and knead lightly. With a lightly floured rolling pin, roll the dough into a 12-inch circle. Transfer the circle to a nonstick pizza pan or baking sheet, gently pulling on the dough to re-form the 12-inch circle.

3 Spread the salsa over the dough; top with the beans, cheese, and onion; then sprinkle with the chili powder. Bake on the bottom rack of the oven until the crust is golden, the cheese is bubbly, and the onion has started to brown, 10–15 minutes. Top with dollops of the sour cream and serve at once.

PER SERVING (¼th of pizza): 395 Cal, 5 g Fat, 2 g Sat Fat, 0 g Trans Fat, 10 mg Chol, 977 mg Sod, 71 g Carb, 7 g Fib, 16 g Prot, 232 mg Calc. **POINTS** value: **8.**

Plan Ahead Double the ingredients and prepare 2 of these pizzas. Freeze the extra one before baking to have on hand for another quick meal. Allow 5–10 minutes extra baking time when you put a frozen pizza in the oven.

1 pound refrigerated or thawed frozen pizza dough
½ cup prepared salsa
1 (15-ounce) can black beans, rinsed and drained
½ cup shredded reduced-fat cheddar cheese
½ onion, chopped
½ teaspoon chili powder
¼ cup fat-free sour cream

Speedy Pizza Margherita

❧❧

Hands-On Prep **10 MIN**
Cook **10 MIN**
Serves **4**

1 Place an oven rack on the bottom rung of the oven. Preheat the oven to 450°F.

2 Spread the tomato sauce over the crust and sprinkle with the cheese. Drizzle with the oil and then sprinkle with the parsley, oregano, basil, salt, and crushed red pepper. Bake on the bottom rack of the oven until the cheese is bubbly, 10–15 minutes.

PER SERVING (¼th of pizza): 260 Cal, 7 g Fat, 1 g Sat Fat, 0 g Trans Fat, 4 mg Chol, 916 mg Sod, 37 g Carb, 2 g Fib, 10 g Prot, 268 mg Calc. *POINTS* value: **5.**

Good Idea One of the secrets of a great pizza is a very hot oven. Be sure your oven has reached the recommended temperature before you slide the pie in.

¾ **cup prepared fat-free tomato sauce**
1 **(10-ounce) thin prebaked pizza crust**
¼ **cup shredded part-skim mozzarella cheese**
2 **teaspoons olive oil**
1 **tablespoon chopped flat-leaf parsley**
½ **tablespoon chopped fresh oregano, or ½ teaspoon dried**
½ **tablespoon chopped fresh basil, or ½ teaspoon dried**
¼ **teaspoon salt**
⅛ **teaspoon crushed red pepper**

Veggie and Cheddar Pizza

❧

Hands-On Prep **15 MIN**
Cook **10 MIN**
Serves **4**

1 Place an oven rack on the bottom rung of the oven. Preheat the oven to 500°F.

2 Sprinkle a work surface lightly with flour. Turn the dough onto the surface and knead lightly. With a lightly floured rolling pin, roll the dough into a 12-inch circle. Transfer the circle to a nonstick pizza pan or baking sheet, gently pulling on the dough to re-form the 12-inch circle.

3 Sprinkle the cheese over the dough; top with the broccoli, mushrooms, salt, and pepper. Bake on the bottom rack of the oven until the crust is golden, the cheese is bubbly, and the mushrooms are cooked through, 10–15 minutes.

1 pound refrigerated or thawed frozen pizza dough
1 cup shredded reduced-fat cheddar cheese
1 (10-ounce) box frozen chopped broccoli, thawed and squeezed dry
1 (10-ounce) package fresh mushrooms, sliced
¼ teaspoon salt
Freshly ground pepper, to taste

PER SERVING (¼th of pizza): 383 Cal, 8 g Fat, 4 g Sat Fat, 0 g Trans Fat, 20 mg Chol, 933 mg Sod, 62 g Carb, 5 g Fib, 19 g Prot, 329 mg Calc. **POINTS** value: **8.**

Express Lane For an even quicker pizza, use broccoli florets and sliced mushrooms from the salad bar of a supermarket. Give the broccoli a quick steam in the microwave before using.

Italian Salad Pizza

❦

Hands-On Prep **20 MIN**
Cook **10 MIN**
Serves **4**

1 Place an oven rack on the bottom rung of the oven. Preheat the oven to 450°F.

2 Place the pizza crust on a baking sheet. Arrange the sliced tomatoes on the crust; spray with nonstick spray. Bake on the bottom rack of the oven until the tomatoes are cooked through, 10–15 minutes.

3 Meanwhile, combine the wine, oil, vinegar, garlic clove, oregano, salt, and pepper in a large bowl; let stand until the flavors are blended, about 10 minutes. Whisk vigorously to blend; discard the garlic. Add the arugula, lettuce, endive, carrots, and cucumber; toss to coat.

4 Slide the pizza onto a large cutting board. Top with the salad, sprinkle with the cheese, and serve at once.

PER SERVING (¼th of pizza): 312 Cal, 10 g Fat, 1 g Sat Fat, 0 g Trans Fat, 2 mg Chol, 661 mg Sod, 45 g Carb, 5 g Fib, 11 g Prot, 302 mg Calc. **POINTS** value: **6.**

Good Idea If you have a variety of vinegars in your pantry, reduce the balsamic vinegar to 1 teaspoon and add 1 tablespoon of red-wine, white-wine, or apple-cider vinegar.

1 (10-ounce) thin prebaked pizza crust
6 plum tomatoes, sliced
3 tablespoons dry white or red wine or vegetable broth
4 teaspoons olive oil
4 teaspoons balsamic vinegar
1 garlic clove, bruised
¼ teaspoon dried oregano, marjoram, or basil
¼ teaspoon salt
Freshly ground pepper, to taste
1 bunch arugula, trimmed
2 cups trimmed and torn romaine or Bibb lettuce leaves
1 Belgian endive, sliced
2 carrots, shredded
1 cup chopped seeded, peeled cucumber
2 tablespoons grated Parmesan cheese

ITALIAN SALAD PIZZA

Core Comfort Dinners

CHAPTER 6

MINI-MEATLOAVES; ZUCCHINI AND
GREEN BEAN SUCCOTASH, PAGE 170

Mini-Meatloaves

❧

Hands-On Prep **15 MIN**
Cook **40 MIN**
Serves **6**

✓

1 Preheat the oven to 350°F. Spray a medium baking sheet with canola nonstick spray.

2 Combine the beef, onion, bell pepper, ¼ cup of the ketchup, the mustard, egg, cornmeal, garlic, oregano, salt, and ground pepper, mixing just until blended. Form into 6 (2½ x 4½-inch) oval loaves. Transfer the loaves to the baking sheet. Spread 1 tablespoon of the additional ketchup over the top of each loaf. Bake until an instant-read thermometer inserted into the center of each loaf registers 160°F, 40–45 minutes. Let stand about 5 minutes before serving.

Per serving (1 loaf): 214 Cal, 7 g Fat, 3 g Sat Fat, 1 g Trans Fat, 98 mg Chol, 579 mg Sod, 13 g Carb, 2 g Fib, 26 g Prot, 30 mg Calc. **POINTS** value: **4.**

1½ **pounds ground lean beef (5% fat or less)**
1 **onion, chopped**
1 **small green bell pepper, seeded and chopped**
¼ **cup + 6 tablespoons ketchup**
1 **tablespoon yellow mustard**
1 **large egg, lightly beaten**
2 **tablespoons cornmeal**
1 **garlic clove, minced**
1 **teaspoon dried oregano**
½ **teaspoon salt**
¼ **teaspoon freshly ground pepper**

Good Idea Mashed potatoes are a must if you're planning to serve meatloaf; ½ cup with each serving will increase the **POINTS** value by **2.** Be sure to deduct the **POINTS** from your **weekly POINTS Allowance.**

Beef and Mushroom Meatloaf

❧

Hands-On Prep **10 MIN**
Cook **1 HR 10 MIN**
Serves **6**

1 Preheat the oven to 350°F. Spray a broiler rack with olive oil nonstick spray.

2 Heat the oil in a large nonstick skillet over medium-high heat. Add the onion and garlic; cook, stirring constantly, until softened, 2–3 minutes. Add the mushrooms and cook, stirring, until they release their liquid and begin to brown, 4–5 minutes. Add the broth and bring to a boil. Cook, stirring occasionally, until the liquid almost evaporates, 5–6 minutes.

3 Transfer the mushroom mixture to a large bowl and let cool 5 minutes. Add the beef, egg, oregano, basil, Worcestershire sauce, salt, and pepper; mix just until blended. Transfer the mixture to the broiler rack and form into a 4 x 9-inch loaf. Bake until an instant-read thermometer inserted into the center of the loaf registers 160°F, 60–65 minutes. Let stand about 5 minutes before slicing. Cut into 12 slices.

1 teaspoon extra-virgin
    olive oil
1 onion, chopped
3 garlic cloves, minced
½ (10-ounce) package fresh
    mushrooms, sliced
¾ cup reduced-sodium
    beef broth
1½ pounds ground lean beef
    (5% fat or less)
1 large egg, lightly beaten
1 teaspoon dried oregano
1 teaspoon dried basil
1 teaspoon Worcestershire
    sauce
¾ teaspoon salt
¼ teaspoon freshly
    ground pepper

PER SERVING (2 slices): 191 Cal, 7 g Fat, 3 g Sat Fat, 1 g Trans Fat, 98 mg Chol, 418 mg Sod, 4 g Carb, 1 g Fib, 26 g Prot, 31 mg Calc. *POINTS* value: *4.*

Good Idea Use a mix of shiitake, oyster, and cremini mushrooms instead of the typical white variety in this recipe. You can buy assorted wild mushrooms in convenient packages in many supermarkets, and they'll enhance the flavor of this meatloaf.

Tex-Mex Meatloaf

❧

Hands-On Prep **10 MIN**
Cook **1 HR 5 MIN**
Serves **6**

☑

1 Preheat the oven to 350°F. Spray a 4 x 8-inch loaf pan with canola oil nonstick spray.

2 Combine the beef, ¼ cup of the salsa, the egg white, chili powder, oregano, cumin, and salt in a large bowl, mixing just until blended. Transfer half the mixture to the baking pan. Top with the cheese, leaving a ½-inch border along the edge. Spoon the remaining mixture over the cheese. Spread the top with the remaining ¼ cup of salsa. Bake until an instant-read thermometer inserted into the center of the loaf registers 160°F, 65–70 minutes. Let stand about 5 minutes before slicing. Cut into 6 slices.

1½ **pounds ground lean beef (5% fat or less)**
½ **cup prepared chunky fat-free salsa**
1 **egg white, lightly beaten**
1 **teaspoon chili powder**
1 **teaspoon dried oregano**
¾ **teaspoon ground cumin**
¾ **teaspoon salt**
1 **cup shredded fat-free cheddar cheese**

PER SERVING (1 slice): 191 Cal, 6 g Fat, 2 g Sat Fat, 1 g Trans Fat, 65 mg Chol, 687 mg Sod, 3 g Carb, 1 g Fib, 31 g Prot, 181 mg Calc. *POINTS* value: **4.**

Try It This meatloaf is also tasty prepared with *pico de gallo* (PEE-koh day GI-yoh)—a zesty condiment made with onion, tomato, bell pepper, jalapeño pepper, cilantro, and lime juice—in place of the salsa. Just make sure it's a fat-free variety.

Hearty Stuffed Cabbage

❧

Hands-On Prep **20 MIN**
Cook **1 HR 30 MIN**
Serves **6**

☑

1 Preheat the oven to 350°F. Spray a 7 x 11-inch baking dish with olive oil nonstick spray.

2 Meanwhile, bring a large pot of lightly salted water to a boil. Add the cabbage and cook until tender, 3–4 minutes. Drain in a colander. Rinse under cold running water, drain again, and transfer to a cutting board. Trim the thick ribs from the leaves and set the leaves aside.

3 To make the filling, cook the rice according to package directions, omitting the salt if desired. Transfer to a large bowl. Heat the oil in a medium nonstick skillet over medium-high heat. Add the onion, garlic, and oregano; cook, stirring occasionally, until softened, about 2 minutes. Add the zucchini and cook, stirring occasionally, until tender, about 5 minutes. Stir the vegetables into the bowl with the rice and let cool 5 minutes. Add the beef, egg, salt, and pepper; mix well.

4 Spread ¼ cup of the tomato sauce in the bottom of the baking dish. Place a rounded ½ cupful of the filling on the center of each cabbage leaf. Fold the sides of each leaf over the filling and roll up. Put the rolls, seam side down, in the baking dish. Pour the remaining tomato sauce over them and bake until an instant-read thermometer inserted into the center of each roll registers 160°F, about 50 minutes.

6 large green cabbage leaves
1 (5¼-ounce) package boil-in-the-bag brown rice
1 tablespoon extra-virgin olive oil
1 onion, finely chopped
4 garlic cloves, minced
1½ teaspoons dried oregano
1 zucchini, finely diced
¾ pound ground lean beef (5% or less fat)
1 large egg
¾ teaspoon salt
¼ teaspoon freshly ground pepper
1 (15-ounce) can tomato sauce

PER SERVING (1 roll with about ½ cup sauce): 256 Cal, 7 g Fat, 2 g Sat Fat, 0 g Trans Fat, 67 mg Chol, 768 mg Sod, 31 g Carb, 4 g Fib, 17 g Prot, 55 mg Calc. *POINTS* value: *5.*

Grilled Lamb Chops with Artichoke Relish

───── ⚮ ─────

Hands-On Prep **10 MIN**
Cook **15 MIN**
Serves **4**

☑

1 To make the relish, heat the oil in a medium nonstick skillet over medium-high heat. Add the shallot and 1 teaspoon of the rosemary; cook, stirring occasionally, until softened, 1–2 minutes. Add the artichokes and cook, stirring occasionally, until lightly browned, 3–4 minutes. Remove the skillet from the heat; stir in the lemon zest. Set aside.

2 Combine the remaining 2 teaspoons of rosemary, the salt, and pepper in a small bowl. Rub the herb mixture over both sides of the lamb chops.

3 Spray a ridged grill pan with olive oil nonstick spray and set over medium-high heat. Add the lamb and cook until an instant-read thermometer inserted into the side of each chop registers 145°F for medium, about 5 minutes on each side. Serve at once with the relish.

2 teaspoons extra-virgin olive oil
1 shallot, chopped
3 teaspoons chopped fresh rosemary
1 (14-ounce) can quartered artichoke hearts, drained
1 teaspoon grated lemon zest
½ teaspoon salt
⅛ teaspoon freshly ground pepper
4 (5-ounce) bone-in loin lamb chops, about 1-inch thick, trimmed

PER SERVING (1 chop with ¼ cup relish): 182 Cal, 8 g Fat, 2 g Sat Fat, 0 g Trans Fat, 57 mg Chol, 519 mg Sod, 6 g Carb, 0 g Fib, 20 g Prot, 16 mg Calc. *POINTS* value: *4.*

Food Note If you prefer your lamb chops without the bone, buy 4-ounce boneless loin chops and reduce the cooking time to about 4 minutes on each side for medium.

Pork Tenderloin with Summer Fruit

Hands-On Prep **15 MIN**
Cook **30 MIN**
Serves **4**

1 Preheat the oven to 450°F. Spray a large rimmed baking pan with olive oil nonstick spray.

2 Combine the paprika, cumin, oregano, and ½ teaspoon of the salt in a cup. Rub the spice mixture all over the pork. Put the pork on the pan and roast until an instant-read thermometer inserted into the center of the pork registers 160°F for medium, 30–35 minutes.

3 Meanwhile, heat the oil in a large nonstick skillet over medium-high heat. Add the shallot and garlic; cook, stirring frequently, until softened, 1–2 minutes. Add the nectarines, plums, peach, and the remaining ¼ teaspoon of salt. Cook, stirring occasionally, until the fruit softens slightly, 3–4 minutes. Remove the skillet from the heat; stir in the cilantro.

4 Transfer the pork to a cutting board and cut into 8 to 12 slices. Serve with the fruit.

1 teaspoon paprika
1 teaspoon ground cumin
1 teaspoon dried oregano
¾ teaspoon salt
1 (1-pound) pork tenderloin, trimmed
2 teaspoons olive oil
1 shallot, finely chopped
2 garlic cloves, minced
2 nectarines, pitted and diced
2 plums, pitted and diced
1 peach, pitted and diced
1 tablespoon chopped fresh cilantro

PER SERVING (2 to 3 slices pork with ½ cup fruit): 229 Cal, 7 g Fat, 2 g Sat Fat, 0 g Trans Fat, 63 mg Chol, 483 mg Sod, 18 g Carb, 3 g Fib, 24 g Prot, 22 mg Calc. **POINTS** value: **5.**

Good Idea Serve each guest ⅔ cup cooked couscous with this spicy pork and fruit combo. The per-serving **POINTS** value will increase by **2.**

PORK TENDERLOIN
WITH SUMMER FRUIT

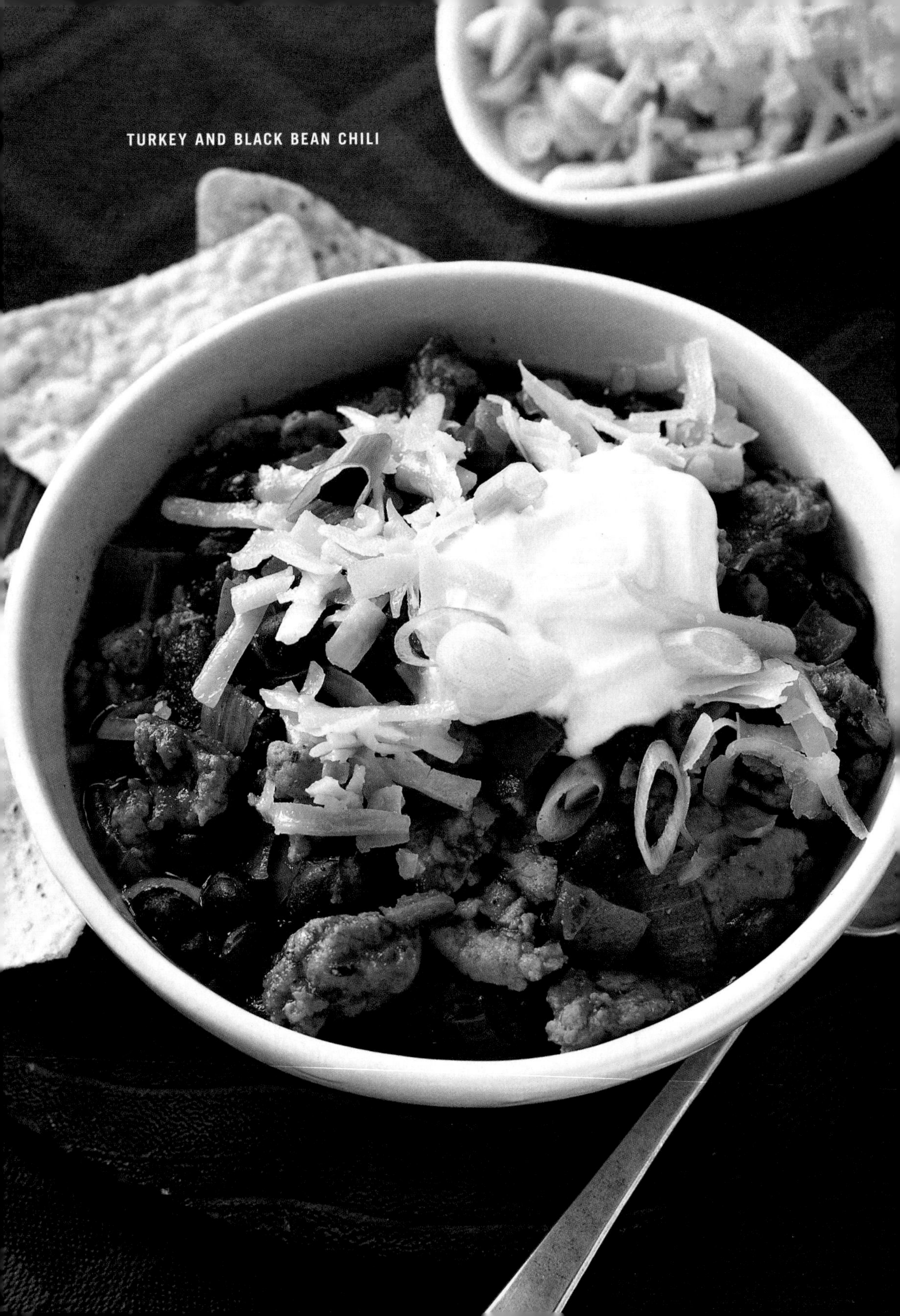

TURKEY AND BLACK BEAN CHILI

Turkey and Black Bean Chili

❧

Hands-On Prep **15 MIN**
Cook **40 MIN**
Serves **4**

Heat the oil in a large nonstick saucepan over medium-high heat. Add the onion, bell pepper, and garlic; cook, stirring occasionally, until softened, about 5 minutes. Add the turkey and cook, breaking it apart with a wooden spoon, until no longer pink, about 3 minutes. Stir in the beans, tomatoes, chili powder, cumin, oregano, and salt; bring to a boil. Reduce the heat and simmer, covered, until the vegetables are very tender, about 30 minutes. Serve with the cheese, sour cream, and scallions.

PER SERVING (1 cup chili with 2 tablespoons cheese, 1 tablespoon sour cream, and 1 tablespoon scallions): 242 Cal, 4 g Fat, 0 g Sat Fat, 0 g Trans Fat, 30 mg Chol, 767 mg Sod, 25 g Carb, 8 g Fib, 27 g Prot, 219 mg Calc. *POINTS* value: *4.*

Plan Ahead This chili tastes even better if made in advance for an instant meal another time. Keep it refrigerated in an airtight container up to 2 days.

2 teaspoons extra-virgin olive oil
1 onion, chopped
1 green bell pepper, seeded and chopped
4 garlic cloves, minced
¾ pound ground skinless turkey
1 (15-ounce) can black beans, rinsed and drained
1 (14½-ounce) can diced tomatoes
1 tablespoon chili powder
2 teaspoons ground cumin
1 teaspoon dried oregano
½ teaspoon salt
½ cup shredded fat-free sharp cheddar cheese
¼ cup fat-free sour cream
¼ cup sliced scallions

Vietnamese Chicken Thighs

Hands-On Prep **10 MIN**
Cook **20 MIN**
Serves **6**

1 To make the marinade, grate the zest from the orange and set aside. Peel the orange, cut into sections, and chop the sections. Combine the orange zest, chopped orange, ginger, soy sauce, and garlic in a zip-close plastic bag; add the chicken. Squeeze out the air and seal the bag; turn to coat the chicken. Refrigerate, turning the bag occasionally, at least 3 hours or overnight.

2 Spray the grill rack with canola oil nonstick spray; prepare the grill.

3 Remove the chicken from the marinade; discard the remaining marinade. Sprinkle the chicken with the salt and pepper and place it on the grill rack. Grill until an instant-read thermometer inserted into the side of each thigh registers 180°F, about 10 minutes on each side.

1 navel orange
**2 tablespoons grated
 peeled fresh ginger**
**2 tablespoons reduced-
 sodium soy sauce**
3 garlic cloves, minced
½ teaspoon salt
**¼ teaspoon freshly
 ground pepper**
**6 (¼-pound) skinless
 bone-in chicken thighs,
 trimmed**

PER SERVING (1 thigh): 129 Cal, 7 g Fat, 2 g Sat Fat, 0 g Trans Fat, 57 mg Chol, 297 mg Sod, 1 g Carb, 0 g Fib, 16 g Prot, 9 mg Calc. *POINTS* value: *3.*

Food Note This Asian-style barbecued chicken can be served hot off the grill or at room temperature.

Seared Scallops with Fresh Corn Relish

Hands-On Prep **10 MIN**
Cook **10 MIN**
Serves **4**

☑

1 Sprinkle the scallops with ¼ teaspoon of the salt and ⅛ teaspoon of the pepper. Heat 2 teaspoons of the oil in a large nonstick skillet over medium-high heat. Add the scallops and cook just until browned and opaque in the center, 3–3½ minutes on each side. Transfer to a plate and keep warm.

2 Heat the remaining 2 teaspoons of oil in the skillet over medium-high heat. Add the onion and garlic; cook, stirring occasionally, until softened, about 2 minutes. Add the corn and cook, stirring frequently, until lightly browned, about 2 minutes. Add the tomatoes and cook, stirring occasionally, until softened, 1–2 minutes. Add the vinegar and cook, stirring constantly, until it evaporates, about 30 seconds. Remove the skillet from the heat; stir in the parsley and the remaining ¼ teaspoon of salt and ⅛ teaspoon of pepper. Serve at once with the scallops.

1½ pounds jumbo sea scallops
½ teaspoon salt
¼ teaspoon freshly ground pepper
4 teaspoons extra-virgin olive oil
1 onion, chopped
3 garlic cloves, minced
1½ cups fresh corn kernels (from 3 ears)
2 plum tomatoes, seeded and chopped
1 tablespoons balsamic vinegar
2 tablespoons chopped fresh parsley

PER SERVING (about 6 scallops with ½ cup relish): 314 Cal, 11 g Fat, 2 g Sat Fat, 0 g Trans Fat, 55 mg Chol, 623 mg Sod, 25 g Carb, 3 g Fib, 31 g Prot, 61 mg Calc. **POINTS** value: **7**.

Play It Safe Avoid purchasing scallops that smell fishy or sour—signs that the mollusks aren't fresh. An excessive amount of milky liquid is a sign of overtreatment with sodium tripolyphosphate. Although this salt is useful in binding moisture to seafood during the freezing and thawing processes, overuse will cause the scallops to soak up additional water.

Shrimp and Pineapple Sauté

Hands-On Prep **15 MIN**
Cook **10 MIN**
Serves **4**

☑

1 Sprinkle the shrimp with ¼ teaspoon of the salt and ⅛ teaspoon of the ground pepper. Heat 1 teaspoon of the oil in a large nonstick skillet over medium-high heat. Add the shrimp and cook just until opaque in the center, about 1½ minutes on each side. Transfer to a plate; set aside.

2 Heat the remaining 2 teaspoons of oil in the skillet over medium-high heat. Add the garlic and ginger; cook, stirring constantly, just until fragrant, about 30 seconds. Add the pineapple and cook, stirring occasionally, until softened, about 2 minutes. Add the bell pepper and cook until it is crisp-tender and the pineapple is lightly browned, 3–4 minutes. Add the shrimp, scallions, lime juice, and the remaining ¼ teaspoon of salt and ⅛ teaspoon of ground pepper. Cook, stirring occasionally, until heated through, about 2 minutes. Serve at once.

- **1 pound peeled and deveined large shrimp**
- **½ teaspoon salt**
- **¼ teaspoon freshly ground pepper**
- **1 tablespoon canola oil**
- **3 garlic cloves, minced**
- **1 tablespoon grated peeled fresh ginger**
- **2 cups cut-up peeled and cored fresh pineapple**
- **1 large red bell pepper, seeded and sliced**
- **3 scallions, cut into 1-inch pieces**
- **2 teaspoons fresh lime juice**

PER SERVING (about 1 cup): 174 Cal, 5 g Fat, 1 g Sat Fat, 0 g Trans Fat, 168 mg Chol, 488 mg Sod, 14 g Carb, 2 g Fib, 19 g Prot, 55 mg Calc. **POINTS** value: **3**.

Good Idea Serve this speedy skillet dish with a side of quick-cooking brown rice; ½ cup cooked rice with each serving will increase the **POINTS** value by **2**.

SHRIMP AND PINEAPPLE SAUTÉ

Healthy
Casseroles

HEARTY SHEPHERD'S PIE

Hearty Shepherd's Pie

Hands-On Prep **20 MIN**
Cook **45 MIN**
Serves **6**

1 Preheat the oven to 350°F. Spray a 2-quart baking dish with nonstick spray. To make the topping, place the potatoes in a large pot with enough cold water to cover; bring to a boil. Cook until the potatoes are fork-tender, 10–12 minutes. Drain; return to the pot. Add the milk, butter, ½ teaspoon of the salt, and ⅛ teaspoon of the pepper; mash and set aside.

2 To make the filling, heat a large nonstick skillet over medium-high heat. Add the beef, breaking it apart with a spoon, and cook until browned, about 5 minutes. Transfer to a bowl. Return the skillet to the heat. Add the onion, garlic, and oregano; cook, stirring, until the onion is lightly browned. Add the wine and tomato paste; cook, stirring occasionally, until the mixture is slightly thickened. Add the peas and carrots; cook, stirring occasionally, until the vegetables thaw. Stir in the broth and cook until the mixture is slightly thickened. Stir in the beef and the remaining ½ teaspoon of salt and ⅛ teaspoon of pepper.

3 Transfer the filling to the baking dish. Spread the potato topping over the filling and bake until the filling is bubbly around the edges, about 20 minutes. Remove the pie from the oven. Increase the oven temperature to broil and broil the pie, 5 inches from the heat, until the topping is lightly browned, 1–2 minutes. Let stand 5 minutes before serving.

1¾ pounds baking potatoes, peeled and cut into 1-inch pieces
⅔ cup fat-free milk
1 tablespoon unsalted butter
1 teaspoon salt
¼ teaspoon freshly ground pepper
1 pound ground lean beef (5% fat or less)
1 onion, chopped
4 garlic cloves, minced
1 teaspoon dried oregano
½ cup dry red wine
2 tablespoons tomato paste
1 (10-ounce) package frozen peas and carrots
1 cup reduced-sodium beef broth

PER SERVING (1⅓ cups): 284 Cal, 6 g Fat, 3 g Sat Fat, 0 g Trans Fat, 47 mg Chol, 557 mg Sod, 34 g Carb, 5 g Fib, 22 g Prot, 72 mg Calc. *POINTS* value: **5.**

Herb-Stuffed Pork Chops

꙳

Hands-On Prep **20 MIN**
Cook **25 MIN**
Serves **4**

1 Preheat the oven to 400°F. Spray a 1-quart shallow baking pan with nonstick spray.

2 To make the filling, combine the bread crumbs, celery, onion, egg substitute, parsley, thyme, and pepper in a medium bowl.

3 Make a pocket in the side of each pork chop by inserting a sharp paring knife into the thickest part and cutting gently back and forth until a large, deep cavity is formed. Fill each pocket with about 2 tablespoons of the filling. Secure the opening with wooden picks.

4 Spray a large nonstick skillet with nonstick spray and set over medium heat. Add the chops and cook until golden brown, about 2 minutes on each side. Transfer the chops to the baking pan. Cover with foil and bake until the pork is no longer pink and the vegetables in the stuffing are tender, about 10 minutes. Uncover and bake until the stuffing is golden and slightly crispy, about 10 minutes longer.

3 tablespoons plain dried bread crumbs
½ celery stalk, finely chopped
½ small onion, finely chopped
2 tablespoons fat-free egg substitute
1 tablespoon chopped flat-leaf parsley
1 teaspoon chopped fresh thyme
¼ teaspoon freshly ground pepper
4 (4-ounce) boneless loin pork chops, trimmed

PER SERVING (1 chop): 208 Cal, 9 g Fat, 3 g Sat Fat, 0 g Trans Fat, 70 mg Chol, 101 mg Sod, 5 g Carb, 1 g Fib, 26 g Prot, 28 mg Calc.
POINTS value: **5.**

How We Did It We retain the great flavor of the pork by browning it on the stove top and finishing it in the oven. This helps to seal in the juices too.

HERB-STUFFED PORK CHOPS

Baked-Bean and Pork Casserole

— ❧ —

Hands-On Prep **20 MIN**
Cook **3 HRS 45 MIN**
Serves **8**

1 Soak the beans according to package directions. Drain.

2 Combine the beans, broth, and water in a Dutch oven; bring to a boil. Reduce the heat and simmer just until tender, 30–40 minutes.

3 Meanwhile, adjust the racks to divide the oven in thirds; preheat the oven to 300°F. Stir the onion, molasses, mustard, chili sauce, and bacon into the beans; return to a boil. (There should be just enough broth to reach the level of the beans; if necessary, add a little water.) Bake, uncovered, on the bottom rack of the oven, 2 hours. Increase the oven temperature to 400°F. Bake until the beans are tender but not mushy and the liquid is thickened, about 1 hour 15 minutes longer.

4 About 20 minutes before the beans are cooked, chop the garlic finely and sprinkle the salt on it; mash to a paste with the side of a large knife. Rub the paste all over the pork. Combine the paprika and Old Bay seasoning in a cup; sprinkle all over the pork. Heat the oil in a large ovenproof nonstick skillet over medium-high heat. Add the pork and cook until browned, 1–2 minutes on each side. Bake on the upper rack of the oven until an instant-read thermometer inserted into the side of each piece of meat registers 160°F for medium, about 10 minutes. To serve, top the beans with the pork.

1 pound dried navy beans, picked over, rinsed, and drained
1 (14½-ounce) can reduced-sodium chicken broth
1 cup water
1 onion, chopped
⅓ cup molasses
5 teaspoons whole-grain mustard
4–5 teaspoons Asian chili sauce
2 slices bacon, chopped
1 large garlic clove
¾ teaspoon salt
1½ pounds pork tenderloin, trimmed and cut into 8 (1½-inch-thick) rounds
1 teaspoon paprika
¼ teaspoon Old Bay seasoning
1 teaspoon olive oil

PER SERVING (generous 1 cup beans with 1 pork round): 379 Cal, 8 g Fat, 2 g Sat Fat, 0 g Trans Fat, 54 mg Chol, 525 mg Sod, 46 g Carb, 10 g Fib, 32 g Prot, 134 mg Calc. **POINTS** value: **7.**

Roast Chicken with 40 Cloves of Garlic

❧

Hands-On Prep **15 MIN**
Cook **1 HR 25 MIN**
Serves **8**

1 Preheat the oven to 375°F. Heat the oil over medium heat in an ovenproof skillet large enough to hold the chicken in a single layer. Add the chicken, skin side down, and cook until browned on all sides, about 5 minutes. Transfer the chicken to a plate.

2 Discard any fat from the skillet and set over medium-high heat. Add the wine, broth, and tomato paste; cook, scraping up the browned bits from the bottom of the skillet. Remove the skillet from the heat; stir in the remaining ingredients. Add the chicken and toss to coat with the sauce. Cover the skillet tightly with foil and bake until the chicken is cooked through and the garlic is softened, 1¼–1½ hours. Remove the chicken skin before eating.

PER SERVING (1 piece of chicken with 5 garlic cloves and 2–3 tablespoons sauce): 158 Cal, 5 g Fat, 1 g Sat Fat, 0 g Trans Fat, 56 mg Chol, 337 mg Sod, 6 g Carb, 1 g Fib, 22 g Prot, 46 mg Calc. *POINTS* value: *3.*

1 tablespoon extra-virgin olive oil
4 (½-pound) bone-in chicken-breast halves
4 (½-pound) bone-in chicken thighs
½ cup dry white wine
½ cup reduced-sodium chicken broth
2 tablespoons tomato paste
40 garlic cloves, unpeeled
½ teaspoon dried rosemary
½ teaspoon dried thyme
1 bay leaf
¾ teaspoon salt
¼ teaspoon freshly ground pepper

Make It Core It's easy to enjoy this French classic if you're following the **Core Plan**. Just omit the wine and increase the chicken broth to 1 cup.

Baked Chicken Parmesan

❧

Hands-On Prep **15 MIN**
Cook **15 MIN**
Serves **4**

1 Preheat the oven to 400°F. Spray a 1-quart shallow baking dish with nonstick spray.

2 Beat the egg and water in a shallow bowl. Combine the bread crumbs, parsley, cheese, and pepper on a sheet of wax paper.

3 Dip 1 piece of chicken into the egg mixture. Then dip both sides into the bread-crumb mixture, shaking off the excess. Place the chicken in the baking dish. Repeat with the remaining pieces of chicken. Discard any leftover egg mixture and bread-crumb mixture. Bake the chicken until golden and cooked through, about 15 minutes.

1 large egg
1 tablespoon water
⅓ cup plain dried bread crumbs
¼ cup chopped flat-leaf parsley
3 tablespoons grated Parmesan cheese
¼ teaspoon freshly ground pepper
4 (¼-pound) chicken cutlets

PER SERVING (1 piece of chicken): 210 Cal, 6 g Fat, 2 g Sat Fat, 0 g Trans Fat, 119 mg Chol, 239 mg Sod, 7 g Carb, 1 g Fib, 29 g Prot, 111 mg Calc. *POINTS* value: *5.*

How We Did It Chicken breasts need to be uniformly thin to cook evenly and quickly. We buy chicken cutlets to save time, or we pound our own skinless boneless chicken-breast halves. To pound, lay a breast between 2 sheets of plastic wrap or put it in a partially sealed zip-close plastic bag (if you seal the bag completely, it will pop). Use a mallet or heavy skillet to pound each breast to a thickness of about ¼ inch.

Crunchy Chicken Bake

Hands-On Prep **15 MIN**
Cook **40 MIN**
Serves **4**

1 Preheat the oven to 400°F. Spray a baking sheet with nonstick spray.

2 Combine the cornflake crumbs, flour, paprika, brown sugar, garlic powder, onion powder, salt, and coriander in a large zip-close plastic bag. Spray the chicken lightly with nonstick spray and place 1 piece in the bag. Shake the bag to coat the chicken evenly; then transfer the chicken to the baking sheet. Repeat with the remaining pieces of chicken, and discard any of the remaining crumb mixture.

3 Bake until the chicken is golden and cooked through, 40–45 minutes.

⅔ **cup cornflake crumbs**
1 **tablespoon all-purpose flour**
2 **teaspoons paprika**
1 **teaspoon packed brown sugar**
¾ **teaspoon garlic powder**
¾ **teaspoon onion powder**
¾ **teaspoon salt**
½ **teaspoon ground coriander**
4 **(½-pound) skinless bone-in chicken-breast halves**

PER SERVING (1 piece of chicken): 244 Cal, 5 g Fat, 1 g Sat Fat, 0 g Trans Fat, 89 mg Chol, 597 mg Sod, 11 g Carb, 1 g Fib, 36 g Prot, 28 mg Calc. *POINTS* value: **5.**

Good Idea Enjoy the chicken hot or cold with a mixed-green salad tossed with your favorite bottled reduced-calorie creamy dressing; 1½ cups greens tossed with 1 tablespoon dressing will increase the per-serving *POINTS* value by **1.**

Citrus Chicken

❧

Hands-On Prep **20 MIN**
Cook **45 MIN**
Serves **6**

☑

1 Preheat the oven to 350°F. Peel off the orange zest with a zester, making sure to avoid the bitter white pith underneath; set aside. Trim off the remaining orange rind with a knife and discard. Cut the orange into 8 wedges.

2 Combine the rosemary, orange zest, oil, paprika, garlic, salt, and pepper in a small bowl. Rub the orange mixture all over the chicken. Transfer to a roasting pan and scatter the orange wedges around the chicken. Roast until the chicken is cooked through, about 45 minutes.

1 orange
1 tablespoon chopped fresh rosemary
1 teaspoon extra-virgin olive oil
1 teaspoon paprika
½ teaspoon garlic salt
¼ teaspoon freshly ground pepper
6 (¼-pound) skinless boneless chicken thighs

PER SERVING (1 chicken thigh): 189 Cal, 8 g Fat, 2 g Sat Fat, 0 g Trans Fat, 77 mg Chol, 155 mg Sod, 3 g Carb, 1 g Fib, 25 g Prot, 33 mg Calc. **POINTS** value: **4.**

Good Idea Juicy chicken thighs are a nice change from the usual breasts and a lot more forgiving of overcooking. Be sure to trim them well, however, as they tend to have a lot of fatty pockets.

Mediterranean Chicken Casserole

Hands-On Prep **15 MIN**
Cook **35 MIN**
Serves **8**

1 Combine the chicken, artichokes, dates, raisins, olives, brown sugar, vinegar, garlic, basil, capers, oil, oregano, salt, and pepper in a large zip-close plastic bag. Squeeze out the air and seal the bag; turn to coat the chicken. Refrigerate, turning the bag occasionally, at least 8 hours or overnight.

2 Preheat the oven to 350°F. Remove the chicken from the marinade and arrange in a single layer in a large roasting pan. Pour the marinade over the chicken; add the broth. Bake until the chicken is cooked through, 35–45 minutes.

PER SERVING (1 chicken thigh with about ½ cup sauce): 287 Cal, 11 g Fat, 3 g Sat Fat, 0 g Trans Fat, 76 mg Chol, 623 mg Sod, 25 g Carb, 3 g Fib, 23 g Prot, 44 mg Calc. *POINTS* value: *6*.

Good Idea As a leftover this casserole is delicious reheated or at room temperature. Be sure to serve it over brown rice to soak up all those delicious juices; ½ cup cooked rice with each serving will increase the *POINTS* value by *2*.

- 8 (¼-pound) skinless bone-in chicken thighs
- 1 (14-ounce) can quartered artichoke hearts, drained
- ¾ cup chopped pitted dates
- ¼ cup raisins
- 12 pimiento-stuffed green olives, halved
- 2 tablespoons packed brown sugar
- 2 tablespoons balsamic vinegar
- 3 garlic cloves, minced
- 1 tablespoon dried basil
- 1 tablespoon drained capers
- 1 tablespoon olive oil
- 2 teaspoons dried oregano
- ½ teaspoon salt
- ¼ teaspoon freshly ground pepper
- ½ cup reduced-sodium chicken broth

Turkey Tetrazzini Bake

Hands-On Prep **15 MIN**
Cook **40 MIN**
Serves **8**

1 Preheat the oven to 375°F. Spray a 7 x 11-inch baking dish with nonstick spray. Cook the spaghetti according to package directions, omitting the salt if desired. Drain and keep warm.

2 Combine the turkey, soup, milk, cheese, garlic powder, cumin, and pepper in a large bowl; add the spaghetti and toss well. Transfer to the baking dish.

3 Combine the bread crumbs and melted butter in a small bowl; sprinkle over the spaghetti mixture. Bake the casserole until the top is golden, 20–25 minutes.

PER SERVING: (1 cup): 261 Cal, 5 g Fat, 2 g Sat Fat, 0 g Trans Fat, 55 mg Chol, 613 mg Sod, 29 g Carb, 1 g Fib, 22 g Prot, 90 mg Calc.
POINTS value: **5.**

- ½ **pound spaghetti**
- 3 **cups cubed cooked skinless turkey breast**
- 2 **(10¾-ounce) cans reduced-fat condensed cream-of-mushroom soup**
- 1 **cup low-fat (1%) milk**
- ⅓ **cup grated Romano cheese**
- ½ **teaspoon garlic powder**
- ½ **teaspoon ground cumin**
- ¼ **teaspoon freshly ground pepper**
- ¼ **cup plain dried bread crumbs**
- 1 **tablespoon unsalted butter, melted**

Good Idea This comfort-food specialty is a tasty way to recycle leftover Thanksgiving turkey. You'll need about 1 pound of cooked turkey breast.

Ginger Salmon en Papillote

Hands-On Prep **20 MIN**
Cook **30 MIN**
Serves **4**

1 Preheat the oven to 425°F.

2 Put the carrots, fennel, leek, and potatoes in a steamer basket; set in a saucepan over 1 inch of boiling water. Cover tightly and steam until the vegetables are slightly wilted but still crunchy, about 2 minutes.

3 Tear off 4 (12-inch) squares of foil. Divide the vegetable mixture in half and then divide one of the halves into 4 equal portions. Place 1 portion on the center of each square. Top each one with a salmon fillet and then with the remaining vegetables. Spoon 2 tablespoons of the hot broth over each portion and drizzle each one with 1 tablespoon of the wine and 1 teaspoon of the oil. Sprinkle with the dill, ginger, salt, and pepper; top with a lemon slice.

4 Fold the foil into packets, making a tight seal. Place on a baking sheet and bake just until the salmon is opaque in the center, about 15 minutes. Open the packets carefully when testing for doneness, as steam will escape.

PER SERVING (1 salmon fillet with 1 cup vegetables): 323 Cal, 11 g Fat, 3 g Sat Fat, 0 g Trans Fat, 75 mg Chol, 454 mg Sod, 28 g Carb, 6 g Fib, 27 g Prot, 89 mg Calc. *POINTS* value: **7.**

- 4 carrots, cut into matchstick-thin strips
- 1 fennel bulb, trimmed and very thinly sliced
- 1 leek, cleaned and thinly sliced (white and light green parts only)
- 2 (5-ounce) Yukon Gold potatoes, peeled and cut into matchstick-thin strips
- 4 (¼-pound) salmon fillets
- ½ cup reduced-sodium vegetable broth, heated
- 4 tablespoons dry white wine
- 4 teaspoons extra-virgin olive oil
- 2 tablespoons chopped fresh dill
- 1 tablespoon grated peeled fresh ginger
- ½ teaspoon salt
- Freshly ground pepper, to taste
- 4 lemon slices

Make It Core To enjoy this elegant dish on the **Core Plan**, omit the wine.

Tuna-Noodle Casserole

Hands-On Prep **20 MIN**
Cook **45 MIN**
Serves **6**

1 Preheat the oven to 350°F. Spray an 8-inch-square baking dish with nonstick spray. Cook the noodles according to package directions, omitting the salt if desired. Drain and keep warm.

2 Meanwhile, combine the soup and milk in a large bowl; set aside.

3 Melt the butter in a large nonstick skillet over medium-high heat. Add the garlic and cook, stirring constantly, just until fragrant, about 30 seconds. Stir in the mushrooms, scallions, peas, thyme, and rosemary. Cook, stirring occasionally, until the mushrooms are softened, about 5 minutes. Stir into the soup mixture. Add the noodles, tuna, and parsley; toss well. Transfer to the baking dish and sprinkle with the potato chips. Bake until the casserole is bubbly and the top is golden, 30–35 minutes.

PER SERVING (1 generous cup): 294 Cal, 7 g Fat, 3 g Sat Fat, 0 g Trans Fat, 61 mg Chol, 601 mg Sod, 38 g Carb, 3 g Fib, 20 g Prot, 102 mg Calc. **POINTS** value: **6.**

Food Note Although we prefer the bright spin that fresh herbs lend to this dish, you can substitute ½ teaspoon each of dried thyme and crushed rosemary in a pinch—but be sure to use fresh parsley.

6 cups extra-wide egg noodles
1 (10 3/4-ounce) can reduced-fat condensed cream-of-mushroom soup
1 cup low-fat (1%) milk
1 tablespoon unsalted butter
2 garlic cloves, minced
½ pound fresh mushrooms, sliced
4 scallions, chopped
1 cup frozen peas
2 teaspoons chopped fresh thyme
2 teaspoons chopped fresh rosemary
2 (6-ounce) cans solid white tuna in water, drained and flaked
¼ cup chopped fresh parsley
1 ounce reduced-fat baked potato chips, lightly crushed (about 1 cup)

Macaroni and Cheese

～ॐ～

Hands-On Prep **15 MIN**
Cook **45 MIN**
Serves **8**

1 Preheat the oven to 350°F. Spray 8 (1-cup) baking dishes with nonstick spray; place on a baking sheet.

2 Cook the macaroni according to package directions, omitting the salt if desired.

3 Meanwhile, melt 2 tablespoons of the butter in a large saucepan over medium heat. Add the onion and cook, stirring occasionally, until softened, about 5 minutes. Add the flour and cook, stirring constantly, about 1 minute. Gradually whisk in the milk. Increase the heat and cook, whisking constantly, until slightly thickened, 3–4 minutes. Whisk in the cheddar cheese, Parmesan cheese, salt, and pepper. Cook, whisking occasionally, until the cheeses melt, about 1 minute.

4 Remove the saucepan from the heat; stir in the macaroni and the tomatoes with their juice. Divide the mixture among the baking dishes. Melt the remaining 1 tablespoon of butter in a small nonstick skillet over medium heat. Add the bread crumbs and cook, stirring constantly, until they are evenly coated, about 1 minute. Sprinkle over the dishes and bake until bubbly and the tops are golden, about 25 minutes.

½ **pound multigrain or whole-wheat elbow macaroni (about 2 cups)**
3 **tablespoons unsalted butter**
1 **small onion, chopped**
2 **tablespoons all-purpose flour**
2 **cups fat-free milk**
2 **cups shredded fat-free cheddar cheese**
⅓ **cup grated Parmesan cheese**
½ **teaspoon salt**
¼ **teaspoon freshly ground pepper**
1 **(14½-ounce) can diced tomatoes with their juice**
¼ **cup plain dried bread crumbs**

PER SERVING (about 1 cup): 246 Cal, 6 g Fat, 4 g Sat Fat, 0 g Trans Fat, 20 mg Chol, 606 mg Sod, 32 g Carb, 5 g Fib, 18 g Prot, 401 mg Calc. *POINTS* value: *5.*

MACARONI AND CHEESE

Snapper with Herbed Bread Crumbs

Hands-On Prep **10 MIN**
Cook **15 MIN**
Serves **4**

1 Preheat the oven to 350°F. Spray a 9 x 13-inch baking dish with nonstick spray.

2 Place the fillets skin side down in the baking dish; sprinkle with the lemon juice. Brush with the oil and then sprinkle with the bread crumbs, capers, salt, and pepper.

3 Bake just until the fillets are opaque in the center, about 15 minutes. Spoon any pan juices over the fillets and sprinkle with the parsley. Serve at once, with the lemon wedges.

PER SERVING (1 fillet): 168 Cal, 6 g Fat, 1 g Sat Fat, 0 g Trans Fat, 60 mg Chol, 388 mg Sod, 5 g Carb, 1 g Fib, 22 g Prot, 40 mg Calc. ***POINTS*** value: *4.*

Good Idea Always use the freshest fish you can find; if red snapper isn't available for this dish, flounder, sole, halibut, catfish, and cod are all excellent choices.

- 4 (¼-pound) red snapper fillets
- ¼ cup fresh lemon juice
- 4 teaspoons olive oil
- 2 tablespoons plain dried bread crumbs
- 2 tablespoons capers, drained
- ¼ teaspoon salt
- Freshly ground pepper, to taste
- ½ cup minced flat-leaf parsley
- 4 lemon wedges

Cheesy Tortilla Casserole

***

Hands-On Prep **20 MIN**
Cook **55 MIN**
Serves **4**

1 Preheat the oven to 375°F. Spray a 1½-quart baking dish with nonstick spray. Stack the tortillas and cut them crosswise into 1-inch strips. Place the strips on a baking sheet in a single layer. Bake until lightly golden, about 6 minutes. Let cool.

2 Spray a large nonstick skillet with nonstick spray and set over medium heat. Add the sweet onion and bell pepper; cook, stirring occasionally, just until tender, about 12 minutes. Stir in the cumin and oregano; remove the skillet from the heat and let the vegetable mixture cool.

3 Meanwhile, combine the creamed corn, eggs, egg whites, ⅓ cup of the cheese, the cilantro, and the pepper sauce in a large bowl. Stir in the vegetable mixture. Spoon about half the mixture into the baking dish. Arrange half the tortilla strips on top. Repeat with the remaining vegetable mixture and tortilla strips. Sprinkle the casserole with the remaining ⅓ cup of cheese. Bake until golden and set in the center, 35–40 minutes. Serve with the salsa.

4 (6-inch) corn tortillas
1 large sweet onion, chopped
1 red bell pepper, seeded and chopped
1½ teaspoons ground cumin
¾ teaspoon dried oregano
1 (15-ounce) can cream-style corn
2 large eggs
3 egg whites
⅔ cup shredded reduced-fat Monterey Jack cheese
2 tablespoons chopped fresh cilantro or parsley
2 tablespoons mild cayenne pepper sauce
¾ cup prepared salsa

PER SERVING (¼th of casserole with 3 tablespoons salsa): 279 Cal, 8 g Fat, 3 g Sat Fat, 0 g Trans Fat, 117 mg Chol, 872 mg Sod, 41 g Carb, 6 g Fib, 17 g Prot, 243 mg Calc. ***POINTS*** value: **5.**

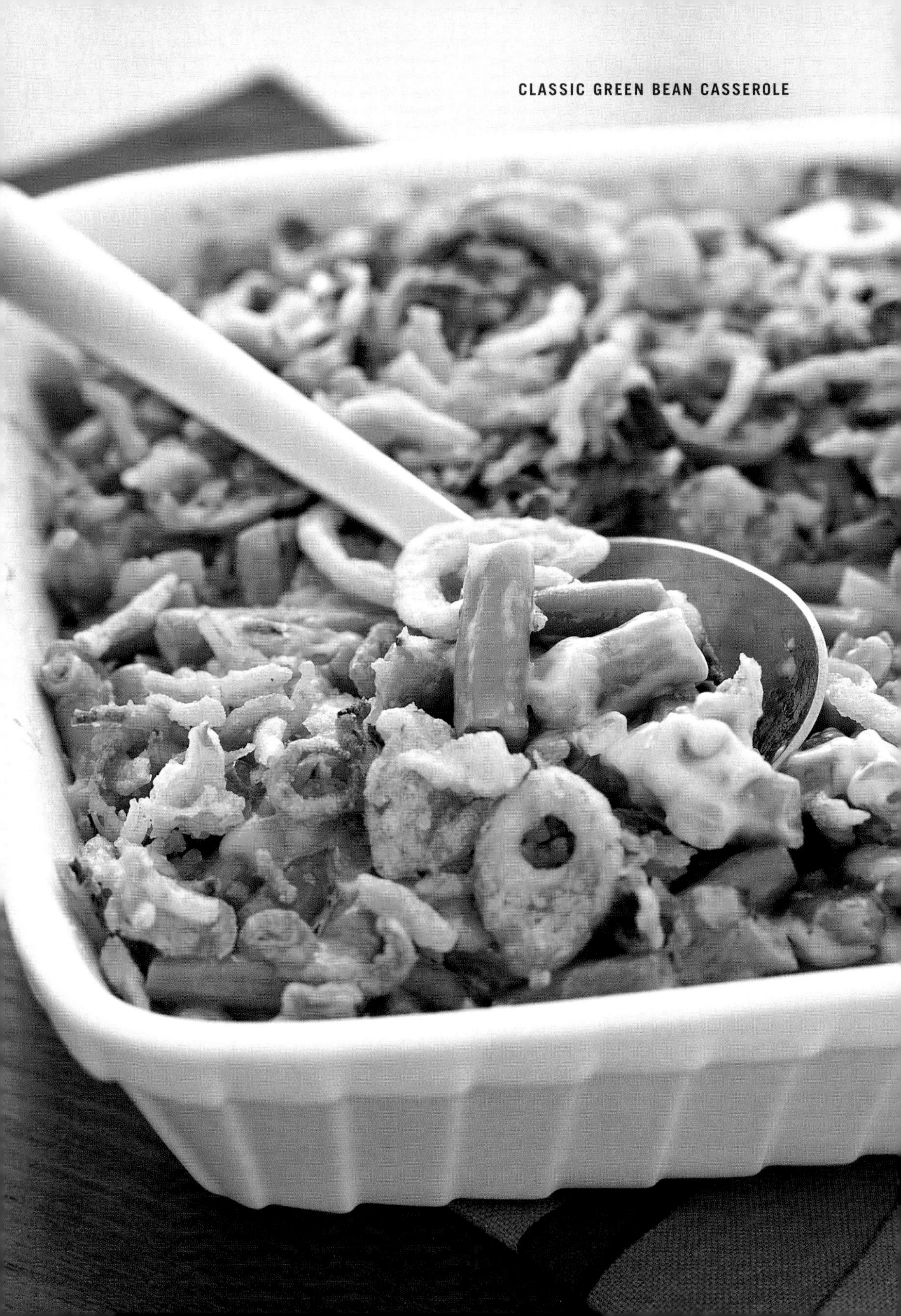

CLASSIC GREEN BEAN CASSEROLE

Classic Green Bean Casserole

❧

Hands-On Prep **10 MIN**
Cook **35 MIN**
Serves **4**

1 Preheat the oven to 350°F. Spray an 8-inch-square baking dish with nonstick spray.

2 Cook the green beans according to package directions. Drain and transfer to a large bowl.

3 Spray a small nonstick skillet with nonstick spray and set over medium-high heat. Add the onion and sugar; cook, stirring frequently, until the onion starts to brown, 5–6 minutes. Transfer to the bowl with the green beans. Stir in the soup, cheese, Worcestershire sauce, and garlic powder. Pour the mixture into the baking dish and bake 25 minutes. Sprinkle with the onions and bake until bubbly, about 5 minutes.

4 cups frozen cut green beans
1 onion, chopped
1 teaspoon sugar
1 (10¾-ounce) can reduced-fat condensed cream-of-mushroom soup
¾ cup shredded fat-free sharp cheddar cheese
1 teaspoon Worcestershire sauce
½ teaspoon garlic powder
¼ cup packaged French-fried onions

PER SERVING (1 cup): 165 Cal, 4 g Fat, 1 g Sat Fat, 0 g Trans Fat, 7 mg Chol, 764 mg Sod, 23 g Carb, 5 g Fib, 11 g Prot, 281 mg Calc. *POINTS* value: *3.*

Good Idea Serve this classic casserole with any of our savory meatloaves—like Beef and Mushroom Meatloaf, page 124, or Tex-Mex Meatloaf, page 125.

Our Best Side Dishes

Twice-Baked Potatoes with Feta Cheese

──────────────── ✦ ────────────────

Hands-On Prep **15 MIN**
Cook **55 MIN**
Serves **4**

1 Preheat the oven to 425°F. Place the potatoes on the oven rack and bake until fork-tender, about 45 minutes. Transfer to a rack to cool slightly; reduce the oven temperature to 375°F.

2 Cut each potato in half lengthwise. Scoop out the flesh, leaving a ¼-inch layer in each shell. Transfer the potato flesh to a medium bowl.

3 Mash the potato flesh with the cheese, yogurt, oil, and chives. Stuff each potato half with a mound of the filling; transfer to a baking sheet. Bake until the filling is hot in the center and the edges are lightly browned, about 12 minutes. Serve at once.

4 small (5-ounce) baking potatoes, scrubbed
⅓ cup crumbled feta cheese, at room temperature
⅓ cup plain low-fat yogurt, at room temperature
1 tablespoon extra-virgin olive oil
1 tablespoon snipped fresh chives

PER SERVING (2 filled potato halves): 194 Cal, 6 g Fat, 4 g Sat Fat, 0 g Trans Fat, 20 mg Chol, 181 mg Sod, 31 g Carb, 3 g Fib, 6 g Prot, 113 mg Calc. **POINTS** value: **4.**

Play It Safe When handling the hot baked potatoes in step 1, be sure to wear oven mitts to protect your hands.

Baked Potato Wedges with Vinegar

Hands-On Prep **10 MIN**
Cook **30 MIN**
Serves **4**

1 Place an oven rack on the bottom rung of the oven. Preheat the oven to 450°F.

2 Halve the potatoes and cut each piece lengthwise into quarters. Toss with the oil in a large bowl.

3 Arrange the potatoes in a single layer on a heavy baking sheet or jelly-roll pan. Bake until the bottoms are deep golden and crisp, about 20 minutes. Turn the potatoes onto the opposite cut side and bake until crisp, about 10 minutes longer. Sprinkle with the salt and pepper and then with the vinegar and serve at once.

PER SERVING (8 wedges with $\frac{1}{2}$ tablespoon vinegar): 154 Cal, 3 g Fat, 0 g Sat Fat, 0 g Trans Fat, 0 mg Chol, 155 mg Sod, 29 g Carb, 3 g Fib, 3 g Prot, 13 mg Calc. *POINTS* value: *3.*

Good Idea A different flavored vinegar will give these crispy potato wedges even more pizzazz. Try white-wine or tarragon vinegar—or even a fruit-infused version, such as raspberry vinegar. If you prefer, serve the vinegar in a small bowl on the side for dipping.

4 small (5-ounce) baking potatoes, scrubbed
1 tablespoon extra-virgin olive oil
$\frac{1}{4}$ teaspoon salt
$\frac{1}{4}$ teaspoon freshly ground pepper
2 tablespoons apple-cider vinegar

Mashed Potatoes with Roasted Garlic

Hands-On Prep **20 MIN**
Cook **55 MIN**
Serves **10**

1 Preheat the oven to 400°F. Cut the top third off
the garlic bulb and discard. Wrap the remaining
garlic in foil and roast until soft and fragrant,
50–60 minutes. Let cool.

2 Meanwhile, place the potatoes in a large pot with
enough cold water to cover by 3 inches; bring to a
boil. Reduce the heat and simmer until fork-tender,
about 20 minutes. Drain the potatoes and return
them to the pot. Mash with a potato masher or fork
until fairly smooth.

3 Squeeze the garlic pulp into a medium saucepan.
Stir in the milk, butter, salt, and cayenne; bring
just to a boil. Reduce the heat and cook, stirring
occasionally, until the butter melts, about 1 minute.
Stir into the potatoes and serve at once.

1 garlic bulb
3 pounds Yukon Gold
    potatoes, peeled and cut
    into 1-inch pieces
⅔ cup low-fat (1%) milk
¼ cup unsalted butter,
    cut up
1½ teaspoons salt
Pinch cayenne

PER SERVING (⅔ cup): 157 Cal, 5 g Fat, 3 g Sat Fat, 0 g Trans Fat,
13 mg Chol, 364 mg Sod, 26 g Carb, 2 g Fib, 3 g Prot, 36 mg Calc.
POINTS value: *3.*

How We Did It By using rich-tasting yellow-
fleshed Yukon Gold potatoes instead of baking
potatoes, we duplicate the flavor of the best mashed
spuds, yet reduce the amount of butter.

Warm German Potato Salad

Hands-On Prep **20 MIN**
Cook **35 MIN**
Serves **4**

1 Place the potatoes in a medium saucepan with enough water to cover by 1 inch; bring to a boil and cook until fork-tender, about 20 minutes. Drain and let cool just until warm. Cut into bite-size chunks and place in a large bowl.

2 Meanwhile, cook the bacon in a medium nonstick skillet until crisp. Drain on paper towels and chop finely. Leave the drippings in the skillet.

3 Add the oil to the skillet and heat over medium heat. Add the red onion and crushed red pepper; cook, stirring, until softened, about 2 minutes. Stir in the broth, mustard, vinegar, and sugar; bring to a simmer. Pour the dressing over the potatoes; toss gently and let stand until some of the dressing is absorbed, 2–3 minutes. Sprinkle with the bacon and serve at once.

1½ **pounds all-purpose potatoes, peeled**
1 **slice bacon**
1 **teaspoon olive oil**
1 **small red onion, very thinly sliced**
¼ **teaspoon crushed red pepper**
¼ **cup reduced-sodium chicken broth**
2 **tablespoons whole-grain mustard**
1 **tablespoon apple-cider vinegar**
1 **teaspoon sugar**

PER SERVING (1 cup): 181 Cal, 4 g Fat, 1 g Sat Fat, 0 g Trans Fat, 2 mg Chol, 162 mg Sod, 34 g Carb, 3 g Fib, 4 g Prot, 24 mg Calc. *POINTS* value: *3.*

Express Lane Skip step 1 and make this dish with cold leftover potatoes. Just warm the potatoes in a microwave before tossing with the hot dressing—the warmth helps the spuds absorb the liquid.

Soyful Potato Gratin

❧

Hands-On Prep **20 MIN**
Cook **1 HR 25 MIN**
Serves **8**

1 Line a baking sheet with a double layer of paper towels. Arrange the tofu in a single layer and top with another double layer of paper towels. Cover with another baking sheet and weight with 2 large cans. Let stand 15 minutes; then pat the tofu dry with more paper towels.

2 Meanwhile, preheat the oven to 400°F. Spray a 2-quart shallow baking dish with nonstick spray.

3 Melt 1 teaspoon of the butter in a large nonstick skillet over medium heat. Add the red onion and cook, stirring occasionally, until tender, about 20 minutes. Add the rosemary. Increase the heat and cook, stirring occasionally, until slightly crisped and golden, 5–7 minutes. Stir in the salt and pepper.

4 Arrange half the potatoes in the baking dish, overlapping them slightly. Top with the tofu, half the onions, and ¼ cup of the cheese. Add the remaining potatoes and top with the remaining onions and cheese. Pour in the broth and dot with the remaining 1 teaspoon of butter. Cover and bake 45 minutes. Uncover and bake until the potatoes are tender and the cheese is melted and slightly golden, about 15 minutes.

½ **pound firm reduced-fat tofu, cut into ½-inch slices**
2 **teaspoons butter**
1 **large red onion, sliced into very thin wedges**
½ **teaspoon dried rosemary**
½ **teaspoon salt**
¼ **teaspoon freshly ground pepper**
1¾ **pounds Yukon Gold potatoes, peeled and cut into ¼-inch slices**
½ **cup coarsely shredded Swiss cheese**
1¼ **cups reduced-sodium chicken broth**

PER SERVING (about ½ cup): 153 Cal, 5 g Fat, 2 g Sat Fat, 0 g Trans Fat, 10 mg Chol, 272 mg Sod, 22 g Carb, 2 g Fib, 8 g Prot, 93 mg Calc. *POINTS* value: *3.*

The Ultimate Creamed Spinach

Hands-On Prep **15 MIN**
Cook **20 MIN**
Serves **4**

1 Put the spinach in a steamer basket; set in a large pot over 1 inch of boiling water (the leaves will be tightly packed but will reduce in volume as they wilt). Cover tightly and steam until bright green, about 2 minutes. Drain in a colander; when cool enough to handle, squeeze out the excess moisture and chop coarsely.

2 Spray a medium nonstick skillet with nonstick spray and set over medium heat. Add the shallots and cook, stirring constantly, until softened, about 3 minutes.

3 Combine the flour, salt, pepper, and nutmeg in a small bowl; stir into the onion. Add the milk and cream cheese; cook, whisking constantly, until blended, about 1 minute. Add the spinach and cook, stirring constantly, just until heated through, about 2 minutes. Serve at once.

1 (10-ounce) bag triple-washed fresh spinach, coarsely chopped
2 shallots, chopped
½ tablespoon all-purpose flour
¼ teaspoon salt
Freshly ground pepper, to taste
Pinch ground nutmeg
¼ cup fat-free milk
¼ cup tub-style light cream cheese

PER SERVING (about ½ cup): 71 Cal, 2 g Fat, 1 g Sat Fat, 0 g Trans Fat, 6 mg Chol, 300 mg Sod, 0 g Carb, 4 g Fib, 5 g Prot, 148 mg Calc. *POINTS* value: *1.*

Zap It Look for spinach in microwavable bags so that you can speed through step 1: Microwave the spinach according to package directions. Carefully cut a slit in the top of the bag (watching out for escaping steam) and transfer the spinach to a colander. When the spinach is cool enough to handle, squeeze out the excess moisture and coarsely chop.

THE ULTIMATE
CREAMED SPINACH

Creamy Cauliflower Puree

❦

Hands-On Prep **10 MIN**
Cook **25 MIN**
Serves **4**

1 Fill a large saucepan two thirds full with water and bring to a boil; add the cauliflower. Reduce the heat and simmer until the cauliflower is soft, about 15 minutes. Drain in a colander.

2 Let the cauliflower cool about 5 minutes; transfer to a food processor or blender and puree in batches if necessary. Add the half-and-half, salt, mace, and pepper; pulse until blended. Serve at once.

**1 (2-pound) cauliflower,
   trimmed and separated
   into florets**
⅓ cup fat-free half-and-half
½ teaspoon salt
⅛ teaspoon ground mace
 **Pinch freshly ground
   pepper**

PER SERVING (½ cup): 45 Cal, 0 g Fat, 0 g Sat Fat, 0 g Trans Fat, 0 mg Chol, 345 mg Sod, 9 g Carb, 3 g Fib, 3 g Prot, 379 mg Calc. ***POINTS*** value: ***0.***

Good Idea You can turn this luscious puree into a creamy soup in a snap. Just heat it with a 14½-ounce can of reduced-sodium chicken broth to make 4 (scant 1-cup) servings; the per-serving ***POINTS*** value will remain the same.

Pizza-Style Cauliflower Bake

❧

Hands-On Prep **15 MIN**
Cook **45 MIN**
Serves **4**

1 Preheat the oven to 350°F.

2 Fill a medium saucepan two thirds full with water and bring to a boil. Add the cauliflower, reduce the heat, and simmer until crisp-tender, 8–10 minutes; drain in a colander.

3 Spread 1 cup of the pizza sauce in an 8-inch-square baking dish or a 9-inch pie plate. Add the cauliflower; then sprinkle with the bread crumbs. Pour the remaining 1 cup of sauce evenly over the top; then sprinkle with the mozzarella and Romano cheeses. Cover with foil and bake until the cauliflower is soft and the cheeses are melted, about 30 minutes.

PER SERVING (about 1 cup): 209 Cal, 9 g Fat, 5 g Sat Fat, 0 g Trans Fat, 18 mg Chol, 849 mg Sod, 21 g Carb, 5 g Fib, 14 g Prot, 326 mg Calc. *POINTS* value: *4.*

Good Idea Crunchy long bread sticks would make an ideal accompaniment to this hearty veggie bake. A pair of 7½-inch sticks with each serving will increase the *POINTS* value by *2.*

1 (2-pound) cauliflower, trimmed and separated into florets
2 cups reduced-fat pizza sauce
¼ cup seasoned dried bread crumbs
1 cup shredded part-skim mozzarella cheese
2 tablespoons grated Romano cheese

Zucchini and Green Bean Succotash

❧☙

Hands-On Prep **20 MIN**
Cook **25 MIN**
Serves **4**

☑

1 Bring a large pot of water to a boil. Add the green beans; return to a boil and cook just until bright green, about 3 minutes. Drain the beans and rinse under cold running water; drain again and set aside.

2 Meanwhile, heat the oil in a large nonstick skillet over medium-high heat. Add the onion and garlic; cook, stirring occasionally, until softened, about 3 minutes. Add the zucchini and tomatoes; cook, stirring occasionally, until softened, about 3 minutes.

3 Stir in the green beans, corn, salt, nutmeg, and cayenne; cook, stirring occasionally, until heated through, about 3 minutes.

PER SERVING (1¼ cups): 152 Cal, 1 g Fat, 2 g Sat Fat, 0 g Trans Fat, 8 mg Chol, 300 mg Sod, 28 g Carb, 5 g Fib, 5 g Prot, 48 mg Calc. **POINTS** value: **3.**

½ **pound fresh green beans, trimmed and cut into 1½-inch pieces**
1 **tablespoon extra-virgin olive oil**
1 **onion, chopped**
1 **garlic clove, minced**
1 **zucchini, quartered lengthwise and cut into ½-inch pieces**
2 **plum tomatoes, chopped**
2 **cups fresh or thawed frozen corn kernels**
½ **teaspoon salt**
⅛ **teaspoon ground nutmeg**
⅛ **teaspoon cayenne**

Good Idea This recipe is great as a summer salad. Prepare as directed except omit the nutmeg. Let the succotash cool; then stir in ¼ cup slivered fresh basil leaves and 1 tablespoon of balsamic vinegar.

Cheesy Corn Pudding

❦

Hands-On Prep **10 MIN**
Cook **45 MIN**
Serves **6**

1 Preheat the oven to 350°F. Spray a 1-quart baking dish with nonstick spray.

2 Place the flour in a medium saucepan. Gradually whisk in the milk. Add the corn, scallions, sugar, salt, thyme, and pepper. Bring to a simmer over medium heat, whisking constantly; cook until slightly thickened, about 2 minutes.

3 Whisk together the egg and egg white in a small bowl. Gradually beat in some of the hot milk mixture, whisking constantly. Whisk the egg mixture back into the saucepan; remove the pan from the heat. Reserve 2 tablespoons of the cheese; stir the remaining cheese into the corn mixture. Spoon into the baking dish and sprinkle the reserved cheese on top.

4 Place the baking dish in a large roasting pan. Set the pan on the oven rack; then carefully pour hot water into the pan, filling it one third full. Bake just until the pudding is set in the center, about 35 minutes. Carefully remove the pudding from the water bath and serve at once.

1½ tablespoons all-purpose flour
1 cup low-fat (1%) milk
2 cups frozen corn kernels
2 scallions, chopped
2 teaspoons sugar
¼ teaspoon salt
¼ teaspoon dried thyme
¼ teaspoon freshly ground pepper
1 large egg
1 egg white
½ cup shredded reduced-fat Monterey Jack cheese

PER SERVING (⅙th of pudding): 115 Cal, 3 g Fat, 2 g Sat Fat, 0 g Trans Fat, 42 mg Chol, 190 mg Sod, 16 g Carb, 2 g Fib, 7 g Prot, 130 mg Calc. **POINTS** value: **2.**

Zap It This is the perfect side dish for a holiday meal. It may be covered with plastic wrap and refrigerated up to 1 day ahead. To reheat, turn back one corner of the plastic to vent and microwave on Medium until heated through, about 4 minutes.

CRUNCHY ONION RINGS

Crunchy Onion Rings

Hands-On Prep **15 MIN**
Cook **15 MIN**
Serves **4**

1 Place an oven rack on the top rung of the oven. Preheat the oven to 400°F. Spray a nonstick baking sheet with nonstick spray.

2 On a sheet of wax paper, combine the flour, salt, and pepper. Place the bread crumbs on another sheet of wax paper. Place the egg substitute in a shallow dish.

3 Coat each double onion ring on both sides with the flour mixture, shaking off the excess. Dip the ring into the egg substitute and then coat it lightly with the bread crumbs. Arrange the rings on the baking sheet (reserving for another use any broken or small inner rings) and lightly spray the tops with nonstick spray. Discard the excess flour mixture, egg, and bread crumbs.

4 Bake on the top rack until browned, about 10 minutes. Turn the rings carefully and bake until browned, about 5 minutes. Serve at once.

2 tablespoons all-purpose flour
¼ teaspoon salt
Freshly ground pepper, to taste
⅓ cup plain dried bread crumbs
¼ cup fat-free egg substitute
2 (½-pound) sweet onions, peeled, cut crosswise into ¼-inch slices, and separated into double rings

PER SERVING (1 cup): 95 Cal, 1 g Fat, 0 g Sat Fat, 0 g Trans Fat, 0 mg Chol, 245 mg Sod, 19 g Carb, 3 g Fib, 4 g Prot, 47 mg Calc. **POINTS** value: *1*.

Good Idea Chop and freeze any unused parts of the onions in a zip-close freezer bag up to 3 months to have on hand when you need chopped onions in a recipe (don't bother thawing them first).

Balsamic Baked Sweet Onions

❦

Hands-On Prep **10 MIN**
Cook **55 MIN**
Serves **4**

1 Preheat the oven to 425°F. Spread the onions evenly in a 9 x 13-inch baking dish; pour in ¼ cup of the water. Drizzle with the oil and vinegar; sprinkle with the sugar, chopped rosemary, salt, and pepper. Cover and bake until tender, about 30 minutes.

2 Uncover and bake until the onions are golden brown and caramelized, about 25 minutes. While cooking, add the remaining ¼ cup of water, and then the final ¼ cup if necessary to keep the onions moist, and baste occasionally. Serve hot or at room temperature. Garnish with the rosemary sprigs (if using).

PER SERVING (about 4 slices): 69 Cal, 3 g Fat, 0 g Sat Fat, 0 g Trans Fat, 0 mg Chol, 149 mg Sod, 12 g Carb, 2 g Fib, 1 g Prot, 24 mg Calc. *POINTS* value: *1.*

1 pound (about 2) Vidalia onions, peeled and cut into ¼-inch slices
½–¾ cup water
2 teaspoons olive oil
2 tablespoons balsamic vinegar
2 teaspoons sugar
2 teaspoons chopped fresh rosemary
¼ teaspoon salt
Freshly ground pepper, to taste
Fresh rosemary sprigs (optional)

Good Idea This delightfully sweet, complex dish makes a lovely accompaniment to Vietnamese Chicken Thighs (page 132).

Puree of Fresh Peas with Mint

Hands-On Prep **20 MIN**
Cook **10 MIN**
Serves **2**

1 Put the peas in a steamer basket; set in a saucepan over 1 inch of boiling water. Cover tightly and steam the peas until bright green, 3–6 minutes.

2 Puree the peas, mint, butter, salt, and pepper in a food processor; add the broth, 1 tablespoon at a time, until the mixture has a thick, creamy consistency. Transfer the mixture to a serving dish and garnish with the mint leaves (if using). Serve at once.

PER SERVING (½ cup): 150 Cal, 6 g Fat, 4 g Sat Fat, 0 g Trans Fat, 16 mg Chol, 126 mg Sod, 18 g Carb, 8 g Fib, 6 g Prot, 38 mg Calc. *POINTS* value: **3.**

1½ **pounds fresh peas, shelled (about 2 cups)**
2 **tablespoons chopped fresh mint**
1 **tablespoon butter**
¼ **teaspoon salt**
⅛ **teaspoon freshly ground pepper**
2–3 **tablespoons reduced-sodium vegetable broth, heated**
Fresh mint leaves or small mint sprigs (optional)

Express Lane Instead of taking the time to shell and steam fresh peas in step 1, microwave a 10-ounce package of frozen peas according to package directions; then proceed with the recipe at step 2.

Roasted Root Vegetables with Herbs

Hands-On Prep **20 MIN**
Cook **40 MIN**
Serves **4**

☑

1 Preheat the oven to 400°F.

2 Combine the carrots, potatoes, turnip, and shallot in a large nonstick roasting pan; drizzle with the oil and sprinkle with the rosemary, thyme, salt, and pepper. Spread the vegetables evenly in the pan.

3 Roast, stirring occasionally, until the shallots are caramelized and the vegetables are browned and tender, about 40 minutes.

PER SERVING (½ cup): 119 Cal, 5 g Fat, 1 g Sat Fat, 0 g Trans Fat, 0 mg Chol, 177 mg Sod, 19 g Carb, 3 g Fib, 2 g Prot, 32 mg Calc. **POINTS** value: **2.**

Good Idea This veggie medley makes a lovely side dish with Grilled Lamb Chops with Artichoke Relish (page 127) or a grilled 4-ounce bone-in lamb chop for a per-serving **POINTS** value of **6.**

2 carrots, cut into chunks
2 (10-ounce) red potatoes, scrubbed and cut into chunks
1 white turnip, peeled and cut into chunks
1 shallot, peeled and quartered
4 teaspoons olive oil
1 tablespoon chopped fresh rosemary
1 tablespoon chopped fresh thyme
¼ teaspoon salt
¼ teaspoon freshly ground pepper

ROASTED ROOT VEGETABLES WITH HERBS

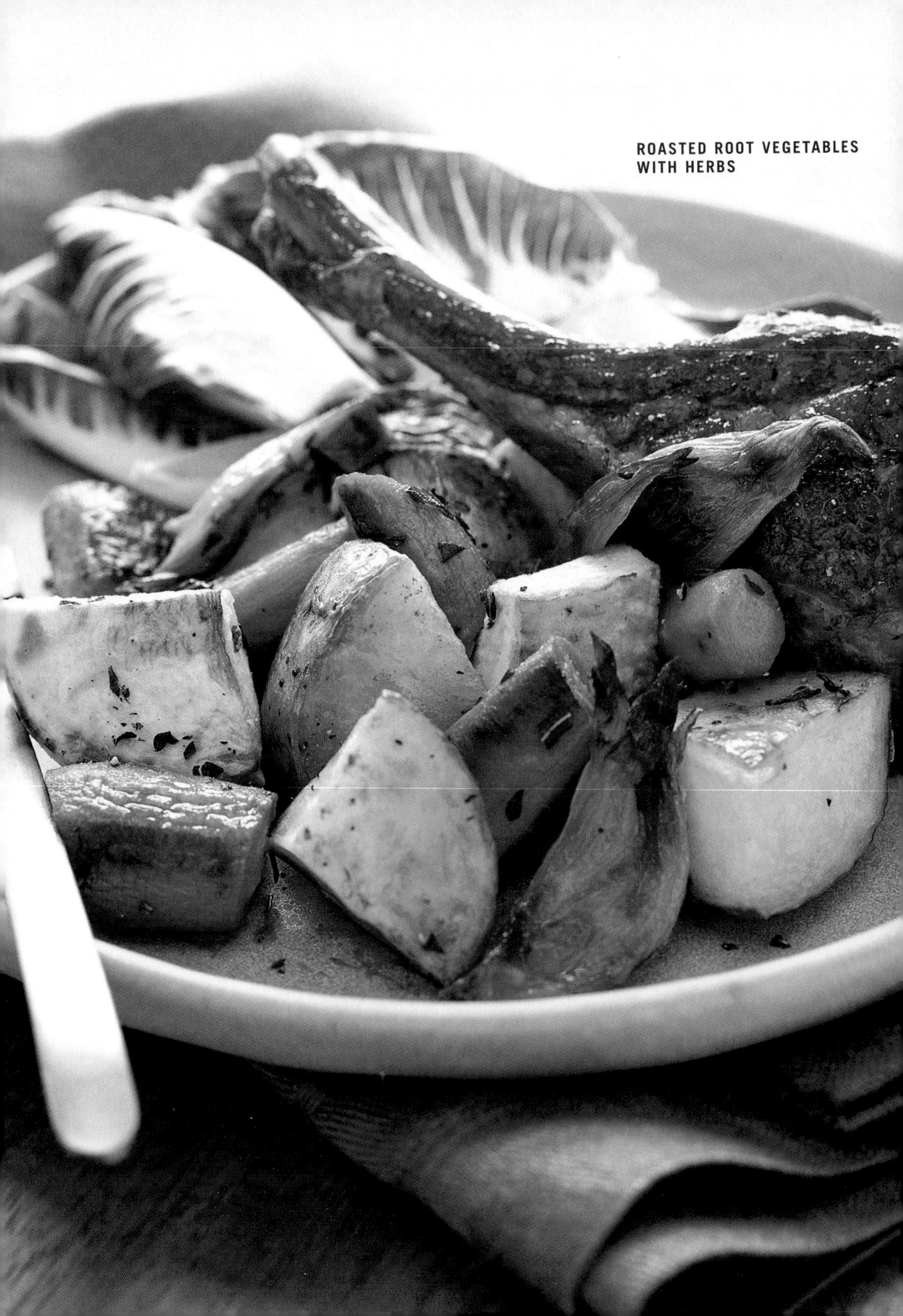

Biscuits, Breads, and Rolls

CHAPTER 9

Whole-Wheat Ice-Box Rolls

❧

Hands-On Prep **25 MIN**
Cook **25 MIN**
Serves **24**

1 Combine the water and honey in a 2-cup measuring cup; sprinkle in the yeast and let stand until foamy, about 5 minutes. Add the oil and egg, stirring until well combined. Combine the all-purpose flour, whole-wheat flour, and salt in a large bowl. Add the yeast mixture and stir with a wooden spoon until a rough dough forms. Turn out the dough on a floured surface; knead until the dough forms a smooth, elastic ball, about 7 minutes.

2 Spray a large bowl with nonstick spray; place the dough in the bowl and lightly spray the top with nonstick spray. Cover the bowl loosely with plastic wrap and refrigerate until the dough doubles in size, at least 8 hours or up to 5 days.

3 Spray 2 large baking sheets with nonstick spray. Punch down the dough. Turn out the dough on a floured surface and cut into 24 pieces. Shape each piece into a ball. Place 12 rolls about 2 inches apart on each baking sheet. Cover loosely with plastic wrap and let rise in a warm spot until doubled in size, 1–1½ hours.

4 Preheat the oven to 425°F. Bake the rolls, one sheet at a time, until golden, 12–15 minutes. Transfer each batch of rolls to a rack. Serve warm or let cool completely.

- 1½ cups warm water (105–115°F)
- 3 tablespoons honey
- 1 package active dry yeast
- 2 tablespoons olive oil
- 1 large egg, lightly beaten
- 2½ cups all-purpose flour
- 1½ cups whole-wheat flour
- 1½ teaspoons salt

PER SERVING (1 roll): 95 Cal, 2 g Fat, 0 g Sat Fat, 0 g Trans Fat, 9 mg Chol, 149 mg Sod, 18 g Carb, 1 g Fib, 3 g Prot, 6 mg Calc. *POINTS* value: *2.*

Multigrain Sandwich Bread

Hands-On Prep **15 MIN**
Cook **35 MIN**
Serves **12**

1 Combine the water, flaxseeds, and honey in a 2-cup measuring cup. Put the whole-wheat and all-purpose flours, yeast, and salt in a food processor. With the machine running, pour the honey mixture through the feed tube; pulse until the dough forms a ball, about 1 minute.

2 Spray a large bowl with nonstick spray; place the dough in the bowl. Cover the bowl loosely with plastic wrap and let the dough rise in a warm spot until doubled in size, 30–40 minutes.

3 Punch down the dough. Turn it out on a lightly floured surface; kneading lightly, form the dough into a loaf. Spray a 5 x 9-inch loaf pan with nonstick spray; sprinkle the bottom and sides with the cornmeal. Place the dough in the pan; cover loosely with plastic wrap and let rise in a warm spot until doubled in size, about 30 minutes.

4 Preheat the oven to 400°F. Brush the top of the loaf with the egg. Bake until deep golden, 18–20 minutes. Cover loosely with foil and bake 15–17 minutes longer. Loosen the sides of the bread with a knife, unmold, and let cool on a rack. Cut into 12 slices.

1¼ cups hot water
   (120–130°F)
¼ cup ground flaxseeds
2 tablespoons honey
2 cups whole-wheat flour
1 cup unbleached
   all-purpose flour
1 package quick-rise yeast
1 teaspoon salt
½ tablespoon cornmeal
1 large egg, lightly beaten

PER SERVING (1 slice): 139 Cal, 2 g Fat, 0 g Sat Fat, 0 g Trans Fat, 9 mg Chol, 199 mg Sod, 27 g Carb, 4 g Fib, 5 g Prot, 19 mg Calc.
POINTS value: *2.*

HERBED BUBBLE BREAD WITH
SUN-DRIED TOMATOES

Herbed Bubble Bread with Sun-Domatoes

Hands-On Prep **25 MIN**
Cook **30 MIN**
Serves **12**

1 Combine the water and sugar; sprinkle in the yeast and let stand until foamy. Microwave the milk, butter, and honey in a microwavable bowl on High until the mixture is warm, 30 seconds. Put the flour and salt in a food processor. With the machine running, scrape the yeast mixture, milk mixture, then the egg, into the feed tube; pulse until the dough forms a ball.

2 Spray a large bowl with nonstick spray; place the dough in the bowl. Cover and let the dough rise in a warm spot until doubled in size, about 1 hour.

3 Combine the thyme and sun-dried tomatoes. Punch down the dough. Sprinkle one third of the thyme mixture over the dough. Fold the dough in half, then repeat twice more to incorporate the ingredients fully. Spray a 12-cup tube pan with nonstick spray. Pull off a golf ball-size piece of dough; shape into a ball and put in the pan. Repeat with the rest of the dough, spacing the balls about ½ inch apart, covering the bottom and then adding a second layer of balls. Cover and let the dough rise until doubled, 45 minutes.

4 Preheat the oven to 375°F. Bake the bread until lightly golden, about 20 minutes. Brush the beaten egg on the top. Bake until deep golden, 10–12 minutes. Unmold the bread on a rack and let cool.

1 cup warm water
   (105–115°F)
Pinch sugar
1 package active dry yeast
¾ cup whole milk
2 tablespoons unsalted
   butter, diced
1 tablespoon honey
4¾ cups unbleached
   all-purpose flour
1½ teaspoons salt
1 large egg
1 tablespoon minced
   fresh thyme or dill
1 tablespoon minced
   drained oil-packed
   sun-dried tomatoes
1 large egg, beaten

PER SERVING (¹⁄₁₂th of loaf): 220 Cal, 3 g Fat, 2 g Sat Fat, 0 g Trans Fat, 32 mg Chol, 310 mg Sod, 40 g Carb, 2 g Fib, 7 g Prot, 32 mg Calc. **POINTS** value: **4.**

Buttermilk Biscuits

~ ❧ ~

Hands-On Prep **15 MIN**
Cook **15 MIN**
Serves **12**

1 Combine the flour, baking powder, salt, and baking soda in a large bowl. With a pastry blender, cut in the butter until the mixture is crumbly. Add the buttermilk to the flour mixture, stirring with a rubber spatula just until moistened. Knead the mixture in the bowl once or twice to form a soft dough. Shape the dough into a disk; wrap in plastic wrap and refrigerate 15 minutes.

2 Meanwhile, preheat the oven to 425°F. Spray a large baking sheet with nonstick spray.

3 On a lightly floured surface, roll the dough to a scant ½-inch thickness. Cut into circles with a 2¼-inch round biscuit cutter, rerolling the scraps to make 12 biscuits. Arrange the biscuits on the baking sheet. Bake until golden brown, 12–15 minutes. Transfer the biscuits to a rack. Serve warm or let cool completely.

1¾ **cups all-purpose flour**
1½ **teaspoons baking powder**
1 **teaspoon salt**
½ **teaspoon baking soda**
5 **tablespoons cold unsalted butter, cut into small pieces**
¾ **cup low-fat buttermilk**

PER SERVING (1 biscuit): 114 Cal, 5 g Fat, 3 g Sat Fat, 0 g Trans Fat, 13 mg Chol, 363 mg Sod, 15 g Carb, 1 g Fib, 2 g Prot, 32 mg Calc.
POINTS value: **2.**

Plan Ahead You can freeze the biscuits in a zip-close plastic bag up to 3 weeks. Remove the biscuits from the plastic bag and reheat from frozen on a baking sheet in a preheated 250°F oven about 10 minutes.

Southern Zucchini-Corn Bread

Hands-On Prep **15 MIN**
Cook **30 MIN**
Serves **12**

1 Preheat the oven to 375°F. Cook the bacon in a large cast-iron skillet until crisp; drain on paper towels and chop. Leave the drippings in the skillet.

2 Combine the bacon, zucchini, buttermilk, creamed corn, cheese, eggs, sugar, chives, melted butter, salt, and pepper in a bowl. Combine the remaining ingredients in another bowl. Add the zucchini mixture to the cornmeal mixture, stirring just until combined.

3 Heat the skillet until very hot, 2 minutes. Remove the skillet from the heat. Scrape the batter into the skillet and spread evenly with a spatula. Place the skillet in the oven and bake the bread until a toothpick inserted into the center comes out clean, about 25 minutes. Loosen the sides of the bread with a knife; let cool at least 10 minutes. Cut into 12 wedges.

PER SERVING (1 wedge): 183 Cal, 5 g Fat, 3 g Sat Fat, 0 g Trans Fat, 45 mg Chol, 405 mg Sod, 28 g Carb, 2 g Fib, 6 g Prot, 126 mg Calc.
POINTS value: *4.*

1½ bacon slices
1 medium zucchini, coarsely shredded (1 cup)
1 cup low-fat buttermilk
1 (8-ounce) can cream-style corn
½ cup shredded extra-sharp cheddar cheese
2 large eggs, at room temperature
3 tablespoons sugar
2 tablespoons snipped fresh chives
1 tablespoon butter, melted
1½ teaspoons salt
¼ teaspoon freshly ground pepper
1¼ cups cornmeal
1 cup all-purpose flour
1 tablespoon baking powder
¼ teaspoon baking soda

Zap It Wrap extra wedges of bread in plastic wrap then place in zip-close plastic bags and freeze up to 1 month. To serve, unwrap and microwave each wedge on Low just until slightly warmed, 30 seconds.

Pumpkin-Poppy Seed Rolls

Hands-On Prep **15 MIN**
Cook **30 MIN**
Serves **12**

1 Put the 2 cups of all-purpose flour, the whole-wheat flour, yeast, sugar, salt, ginger, and allspice in a food processor. Whisk together the milk and pumpkin in a microwavable bowl; stir in the butter. Microwave on High until the butter is melted and the milk registers 120–130°F on an instant-read thermometer, 50–70 seconds. With the food processor running, scrape the milk mixture into the feed tube, followed by 1 of the eggs. Pulse about 1 minute, gradually adding the additional 2 tablespoons of all-purpose flour if needed, until the dough forms a ball.

2 Spray a large bowl with nonstick spray; place the dough in the bowl. Cover and let the dough rise in a warm spot until doubled in size, about 40 minutes.

3 Punch down the dough. Spray a 12-cup muffin tin with nonstick spray. Roll the dough into a cylinder; then cut into 12 equal pieces. Shape each piece into a ball; place a ball in each cup. Cover and let rise in a warm spot until the balls double in size, about 20 minutes.

4 Preheat the oven to 350°F. Beat the remaining egg; lightly brush the tops of the rolls with the egg and sprinkle with the poppy seeds. Bake until golden, about 20 minutes. Immediately remove the rolls from the muffin tin and let cool completely on a rack.

2 cups + 2 tablespoons unbleached all-purpose flour
1½ cups whole-wheat flour
1 package quick-rise yeast
1 tablespoon sugar
¾ teaspoon salt
½ teaspoon ground ginger
¼ teaspoon ground allspice
¾ cup whole milk
½ cup canned pumpkin puree
2 tablespoons butter, diced
2 large eggs
1 tablespoon poppy seeds

PER SERVING (1 roll): 176 Cal, 3 g Fat, 2 g Sat Fat, 0 g Trans Fat, 32 mg Chol, 176 mg Sod, 31 g Carb, 2 g Fib, 6 g Prot, 43 mg Calc. *POINTS* value: *3.*

PUMPKIN-POPPY SEED ROLLS

ORANGE-GLAZED QUICK BREAD

Orange-Glazed Quick Bread

Hands-On Prep **15 MIN**
Cook **40 MIN**
Serves **16**

1 Preheat the oven to 350°F. Spray a 5 x 9-inch loaf pan with nonstick spray and dust with flour.

2 Combine the flour, baking powder, baking soda, nutmeg, and salt in a large bowl. Whisk together the granulated sugar, orange juice, oil, eggs, orange zest, and vanilla in another bowl. Add the sugar mixture to the flour mixture, stirring until well combined. Pour the batter into the pan. Bake until a toothpick inserted into the center of the bread comes out clean, 40–45 minutes. Cool in the pan on a rack 10 minutes. Remove the bread from the pan and cool completely on the rack.

3 To make the glaze, whisk together all the ingredients in a medium bowl until smooth. With a spatula, spread the glaze evenly over the top of the cooled bread. Let stand until the glaze sets, about 10 minutes. Cut into 16 slices.

2 cups all-purpose flour
1 teaspoon baking powder
½ teaspoon baking soda
¼ teaspoon ground nutmeg
¼ teaspoon salt
1 cup granulated sugar
½ cup orange juice
⅓ cup canola oil
2 large eggs
2 teaspoons grated
orange zest
1 teaspoon vanilla extract

GLAZE
¾ cup confectioners' sugar
2 tablespoons orange juice
½ teaspoon grated
orange zest

PER SERVING (1 slice): 183 Cal, 5 g Fat, 1 g Sat Fat, 0 g Trans Fat, 27 mg Chol, 108 mg Sod, 31 g Carb, 1 g Fib, 3 g Prot, 12 mg Calc. *POINTS* value: **4.**

Good Idea For a great dessert, try topping a slice of this citrusy bread with vanilla or chocolate fat-free frozen yogurt. A ¼-cup scoop will increase the per-serving *POINTS* value by *1.*

Perfect Pies and Other Sweets

Classic Southern Ambrosia

❧

Hands-On Prep **15 MIN**
Cook **NONE**
Serves **6**

1 Trim the rind and white pith from the oranges; then cut each orange in half lengthwise. Slice the orange halves crosswise into ¼-inch-thick half rounds; transfer to a large bowl, along with any juice. Add the pineapple, apple, grapes, coconut, and honey; toss to combine. Cover and refrigerate up to 1 day if desired.

2 When ready to serve, gently toss the fruit mixture and transfer to a serving dish. Sprinkle with the walnuts and serve at once.

PER SERVING (about ½ cup): 139 Cal, 3 g Fat, 1 g Sat Fat, 0 g Trans Fat, 0 mg Chol, 12 mg Sod, 29 g Carb, 3 g Fib, 1 g Prot, 27 mg Calc. *POINTS* value: *2.*

2 navel oranges
1½ cups cubed peeled and cored fresh pineapple
1 red apple, chopped
1 cup seedless grapes, halved if large
¼ cup shredded sweetened coconut
3 tablespoons honey
2 tablespoons toasted and finely chopped walnuts

How We Did It To toast the walnuts, we placed them in a dry nonstick skillet over medium heat. We cooked them, shaking the pan frequently, until the nuts became fragrant and only slightly darkened (being careful not to burn them), about 3 minutes.

Triple-Cranberry Baked Apples

❦

Hands-On Prep **20 MIN**
Cook **40 MIN**
Serves **4**

1 Preheat the oven to 375°F. Combine the cranberry juice and 2 tablespoons of the brown sugar in the bottom of a 1½-quart baking dish.

2 Using an apple corer or melon baller, cut out the cores of the apples without cutting them through to the bottom. Peel the top halves of the apples. Trim the bottoms if necessary so that they stand upright.

3 Combine the fresh and dried cranberries, ginger, the remaining 2 tablespoons of brown sugar, the cinnamon, and allspice in a small bowl. Pack the mixture into the cavities of the apples. Place the apples in the baking dish and cover loosely with foil. Bake, occasionally spooning the pan juices over the apples, just until the apples are tender when pierced with a knife, 40–45 minutes. Transfer the baking dish to a rack and let cool.

4 Meanwhile, combine the sour cream and vanilla in a small bowl. Just before serving, baste the apples with the pan juices. Serve with extra pan juices on the side and a dollop of the sour cream mixture.

1 cup cranberry juice
4 tablespoons packed light brown sugar
4 large baking apples (1½ pounds), such as Jonagold, McIntosh, or Gala
½ cup fresh or frozen cranberries, coarsely chopped
⅓ cup dried cranberries
1 tablespoon chopped crystallized ginger
½ teaspoon cinnamon
¼ teaspoon ground allspice
3 tablespoons fat-free sour cream
½ teaspoon vanilla extract

PER SERVING (1 apple with 2½ tablespoons juices and about 2 teaspoons sour cream): 270 Cal, 1 g Fat, 0 g Sat Fat, 0 g Trans Fat, 1 mg Chol, 16 mg Sod, 69 g Carb, 7 g Fib, 1 g Prot, 54 mg Calc. *POINTS* value: **5.**

Spiced Plum Compote

❧

Hands-On Prep **15 MIN**
Cook **25 MIN**
Serves **6**

1 Place the cinnamon sticks, ginger, peppercorns, and whole allspice in the center of a 5-inch square of cheesecloth. Gather up the edges of the cheesecloth and tie them together with kitchen string. Place in a medium saucepan; add the brown sugar, port, and cranberry juice. Cover and bring to a simmer over medium heat; reduce the heat and simmer 10 minutes.

2 Meanwhile, slice each plum half into thirds. Add to the saucepan, return to a simmer, and cook, covered, until the plums have softened 10–12 minutes. Remove the pan from the heat, stir in the lemon juice, and let cool. Transfer the compote to a bowl and refrigerate until chilled, at least 2 hours or up to 5 days. Remove the spice bag before serving. Serve the compote chilled or at room temperature.

2 (3-inch) cinnamon sticks
4 slices peeled fresh ginger
8 whole black peppercorns
5 whole allspice berries
½ cup packed dark brown sugar
½ cup ruby port
½ cup cranberry juice
1½ pounds fresh plums (about 9 medium), halved and pitted
1 tablespoon fresh lemon juice

PER SERVING (scant ½ cup): 171 Cal, 1 g Fat, 0 g Sat Fat, 0 g Trans Fat, 0 mg Chol, 10 mg Sod, 37 g Carb, 2 g Fib, 1 g Prot, 22 mg Calc. **POINTS** value: **3.**

Food Note If you prefer an alcohol-free version of this homey dessert, substitute orange juice or extra cranberry juice for the port.

Berry-Nectarine Cobbler

❧

Hands-On Prep **20 MIN**
Cook **30 MIN**
Serves **6**

1 Preheat the oven to 375°F. Whisk together the jam, cranberry juice, cornstarch, ginger, and allspice in a 9-inch deep-dish microwavable pie plate or casserole dish until blended. Stir in the nectarines to coat well. Microwave on High, stirring occasionally, until the mixture begins to bubble, 6–7 minutes.

2 Meanwhile, to make the topping, whisk together the flour, 2 tablespoons of the sugar, the baking powder, and baking soda in a medium bowl. Make a well in the center and pour the buttermilk and melted butter into it. Quickly combine the flour and buttermilk mixtures, stirring just until blended. Drop the topping by tablespoonfuls on the hot fruit, forming 6 mounds. Sprinkle the top with the remaining 1 tablespoon of sugar. Bake until the biscuits are golden and the fruit mixture is bubbly, about 25 minutes. Serve warm.

- ½ **cup raspberry jam**
- ⅓ **cup cranberry juice**
- 1 **tablespoon cornstarch**
- ½ **teaspoon ground ginger**
- ¼ **teaspoon ground allspice**
- 1½ **pounds firm-ripe nectarines, halved, pitted, and thinly sliced**
- 1 **cup all-purpose flour**
- 3 **tablespoons sugar**
- 1 **teaspoon baking powder**
- ¼ **teaspoon baking soda**
- ½ **cup low-fat buttermilk**
- 2 **tablespoons melted unsalted butter**

PER SERVING (⅙th of cobbler): 247 Cal, 4 g Fat, 3 g Sat Fat, 0 g Trans Fat, 11 mg Chol, 167 mg Sod, 51 g Carb, 3 g Fib, 4 g Prot, 85 mg Calc. *POINTS* value: *5.*

Food Note If you want to use fresh peaches instead of nectarines, we suggest you peel them. Plunge them into boiling water just long enough to loosen their skins, 1 to 3 minutes. Then transfer them to a bowl of ice water. When they are cool enough to handle, the skins will slip off easily.

No-Bake Strawberry-Rhubarb Crumble

❧

Hands-On Prep **20 MIN**
Cook **15 MIN**
Serves **6**

1 Combine the sugar and cornstarch in a medium saucepan. Stir in the rhubarb, water, orange zest, and ginger. Bring to a simmer, covered, over medium heat. Cook, stirring occasionally, until the rhubarb is tender and the sauce has thickened, about 8 minutes. Stir in the strawberries and cook 2 minutes longer. Pour into a 9-inch pie plate or serving dish.

2 To make the topping, chop the cookies into ¼-inch pieces and place in a medium bowl. Crumble in the brown sugar and add the allspice. Drizzle in the melted butter and stir to distribute evenly. Just before serving, sprinkle the topping over the fruit. Serve the crumble warm or at room temperature.

½ cup sugar
1½ tablespoons cornstarch
1½ cups sliced fresh or
    frozen rhubarb
½ cup water
1 teaspoon grated
    orange zest
½ teaspoon ground ginger
2 cups hulled and halved
    fresh strawberries
3 almond-toast cookies
    (1½ ounces)
1 tablespoon packed dark
    brown sugar
⅛ teaspoon allspice
1 tablespoon unsalted
    butter, melted

PER SERVING (⅙th of crumble): 142 Cal, 3 g Fat, 0 g Trans Fat, 1 g Sat Fat, 6 mg Chol, 28 mg Sod, 30 g Carb, 2 g Fib, 1 g Prot, 75 mg Calc. **POINTS** value: **3.**

Good Idea Serve this old-fashioned "spoon pie" with a small scoop of vanilla fat-free frozen yogurt; ¼ cup will increase the per-serving **POINTS** value by **1.**

Fruited Bread Pudding

Hands-On Prep **20 MIN**
Cook **1 HR**
Serves **8**

1 Bring the apricots, water, and bourbon to a simmer in a small saucepan over medium heat. Remove from the heat, stir in the pear, and let cool.

2 Spray a 9 x 11-inch baking dish with nonstick spray. Scatter the bread in the pan in an even layer. Spoon the fruit mixture evenly on top. Whisk together the granulated sugar, cinnamon, and nutmeg in a medium bowl. Whisk in the milk, eggs, egg white, vanilla, and lemon zest. Pour over the bread, pressing down on the cubes so that they soak up the liquid. Cover with foil and let stand 30 minutes.

3 Preheat the oven to 350°F. Place the baking dish in a large roasting pan. Place the pan in the oven; then carefully pour hot water into the pan, filling it halfway. Bake 30 minutes. Uncover and bake until puffed and golden, about 30 minutes. Carefully remove the baking dish from the water bath. Serve warm, sifting the confectioners' sugar on top.

- ¾ **cup dried apricots, diced**
- 3 **tablespoons water**
- 2 **tablespoons bourbon**
- 1 **ripe pear, peeled, quartered, and sliced crosswise**
- 4 **cups (1-inch) cubes day-old whole-grain bread**
- ½ **cup granulated sugar**
- ¾ **teaspoon cinnamon**
- ¼ **teaspoon ground nutmeg**
- 3 **cups low-fat (1%) milk**
- 2 **large eggs**
- 1 **egg white**
- 2 **teaspoons vanilla extract**
- 1 **teaspoon grated lemon zest**
- 2 **tablespoons confectioners' sugar**

PER SERVING (⅛th of pudding): 197 Cal, 3 g Fat, 1 g Sat Fat, 0 g Trans Fat, 57 mg Chol, 161 mg Sod, 37 g Carb, 3 g Fib, 7 g Prot, 142 mg Calc. *POINTS* value: *4.*

Plan Ahead To get a jump-start on the prep, follow steps 1 to 3 and refrigerate the mixture overnight. Then complete the pudding as directed the next day.

DOUBLE-CHOCOLATE FONDUE

Double-Chocolate Fondue

❧

Hands-On Prep **15 MIN**
Cook **10 MIN**
Serves **12**

1 Whisk together the whole milk, evaporated milk, and cocoa powder in a medium saucepan until the cocoa powder dissolves. Add the chocolate and cook over medium-low heat, stirring constantly, until the chocolate is melted and the mixture is smooth, 3–5 minutes.

2 Stir in the sugar, water, and corn syrup. Cook, stirring constantly, until the mixture is smooth, 4–6 minutes. Transfer to a fondue pot and set over medium heat. Serve at once, with the strawberries for dipping.

PER SERVING (scant 3 tablespoons fondue with 4 strawberries): 176 Cal, 7 g Fat, 4 g Sat Fat, 0 g Trans Fat, 1 mg Chol, 22 mg Sod, 33 g Carb, 3 g Fib, 8 g Prot, 59 mg Calc. **POINTS** value: **4.**

⅓ **cup whole milk**
½ **cup evaporated**
  fat-free milk
¾ **cup unsweetened**
  cocoa powder
6 **ounces semisweet**
  chocolate, chopped
1 **cup sugar**
¼ **cup water**
2 **tablespoons light**
  corn syrup
4 **dozen fresh strawberries,**
  stemmed

Good Idea For true indulgence, serve this fondue with a 1-ounce piece of prepared fat-free angel food cake cut into 1-inch cubes, along with the strawberries. The per-serving **POINTS** value will increase by *1*.

Classic Bananas Foster

❧

Hands-On Prep **10 MIN**
Cook **10 MIN**
Serves **4**

1 Combine the brown sugar, butter, and nutmeg in a large nonstick skillet. Cook over medium-low heat, stirring frequently, until the butter melts and the sugar dissolves, about 5 minutes. Add the bananas and cook, tossing to coat, until the bananas begin to soften, 2–4 minutes. Increase the heat to medium, remove the skillet from the heat, and pour in the rum. Return the skillet to the heat and ignite the rum with a long wooden match; cook, shaking the pan, until the flame goes out, about 30 seconds. Continue cooking until the sauce thickens slightly, about 1 minute. Remove the skillet from the heat.

2 Place a scoop of frozen yogurt into each of 4 serving dishes. Top each scoop with warm banana mixture and serve at once.

PER SERVING (¼ cup frozen yogurt with ½ cup banana mixture): 218 Cal, 5 g Fat, 3 g Sat Fat, 0 g Trans Fat, 16 mg Chol, 40 mg Sod, 43 g Carb, 2 g Fib, 4 g Prot, 107 mg Calc. *POINTS* value: **4.**

⅓ **cup packed dark brown sugar**
3 **tablespoons unsalted light butter**
½ **teaspoon ground nutmeg**
2 **large ripe bananas, peeled and cut into ¼-inch slices**
2 **tablespoons dark rum**
½ **pint vanilla fat-free frozen yogurt**

Food Note If you'd rather skip the rum—and the flames—substitute 1 teaspoon imitation rum extract or add 2 tablespoons pineapple juice and a few drops of vanilla extract with the bananas.

Blueberry Mini-Cheesecakes

Hands-On Prep **20 MIN**
Cook **10 MIN**
Serves **12**

1 Preheat the oven to 375°F. Line 24 mini–muffin cups with paper liners; spray the liners with nonstick spray. Microwave the honey in a medium microwavable bowl on High until warm, about 10 seconds. Add the gingersnap crumbs; mix well. Spoon 1 scant teaspoon of the crumb mixture into the bottom of each muffin cup.

2 With an electric mixer on high speed, beat the cream cheese, sugar, egg, orange zest, and almond extract in a bowl until fluffy, about 3 minutes. Spoon 1 level tablespoon of the mixture into each muffin cup. Bake until cakes are puffed and set in the center, about 9 minutes. Cool in the pans on a rack.

3 Microwave the jam in a medium microwavable bowl on High just until it begins to bubble, about 15 seconds. Gently stir in the blueberries until evenly coated. Spoon 5–6 blueberries over each cheesecake. Refrigerate until ready to serve.

2 teaspoons honey
8 gingersnaps, crushed to fine crumbs (about ½ cup)
1 (8-ounce) package light cream cheese (Neufchâtel), at room temperature
¼ cup sugar
1 large egg
1 teaspoon grated orange zest
¼ teaspoon almond extract
¼ cup all-fruit blueberry jam
1 cup fresh blueberries

PER SERVING (2 mini-cheesecakes): 117 Cal, 5 g Fat, 3 g Sat Fat, 0 g Trans Fat, 32 mg Chol, 108 mg Sod, 15 g Carb, 1 g Fib, 3 g Prot, 21 mg Calc. **POINTS** value: **3.**

Plan Ahead Prepare the cheesecakes through step 2 up to 2 days ahead and store in the refrigerator; they taste even better with a day's chilling. The topping can be assembled in minutes just before serving.

Panna Cotta with Berry Sauce

❦

Hands-On Prep **20 MIN**
Cook **5 MIN**
Serves **4**

1 Pour the water into a small bowl and sprinkle with the gelatin. Let stand until the gelatin is softened, about 5 minutes.

2 Meanwhile, combine the cream and the ¼ cup of sugar in a medium saucepan. Cook over medium heat, stirring occasionally, until the sugar dissolves, about 5 minutes. Remove the pan from the heat; add the gelatin mixture, stirring until dissolved. Add the yogurt and vanilla and almond extracts, stirring until smooth. Divide the mixture among 4 (½-cup) custard cups. Cover the cups and refrigerate until set, at least 4 hours or overnight.

3 To make the berry sauce, place the raspberries, the additional 1 tablespoon sugar, and lemon juice in a blender and puree. Strain through a fine sieve into a bowl; discard the seeds and stir in the lemon zest. Cover and refrigerate until ready to use.

4 To serve, run a thin-bladed knife around the edge of each custard cup; then dip the cups into a bowl of hot water, holding them there about 15 seconds. Immediately invert the cups onto a plate. Top each one with 1 tablespoon of the sauce.

2 tablespoons water
1 teaspoon unflavored gelatin
6 tablespoons heavy cream
¼ cup + 1 tablespoon sugar
1 cup vanilla fat-free yogurt
½ teaspoon vanilla extract
¼ teaspoon almond extract
2 cups fresh or thawed frozen raspberries
1 teaspoon fresh lemon juice
½ teaspoon grated lemon zest

PER SERVING (1 custard with 1 tablespoon sauce): 202 Cal, 7 g Fat, 4 g Sat Fat, 0 g Trans Fat, 26 mg Chol, 35 mg Sod, 32 g Carb, 4 g Fib, 4 g Prot, 111 mg Calc. *POINTS* value: **4.**

Classic Crêpes Suzette

Hands-On Prep **20 MIN**
Cook **15 MIN**
Serves **6**

1 Combine the flour, 1 tablespoon of the sugar, and the salt in a medium bowl. Combine the milk, eggs, and orange zest in another bowl. Gradually whisk the milk mixture into the flour mixture until blended; let stand 15 minutes.

2 Spray a small nonstick skillet or crêpe pan with nonstick spray and set over medium heat. When a drop of water sizzles on the skillet, stir the batter, pour a scant ¼ cupful onto it, and swirl to coat. Cook the crêpe until the underside is set, 1–2 minutes. Flip and cook through on the other side, about 15 seconds longer. Slide the crêpe onto a plate. Repeat with the remaining batter, making a total of 6 crêpes. Cover loosely with plastic wrap and set aside.

3 Combine the orange juice, the orange segments and their juice, and the remaining 3 tablespoons of the sugar in a large skillet. Cook over medium heat, stirring occasionally, until the sugar dissolves, about 2 minutes. Working one at a time, dip each crêpe into the hot juice mixture. Fold each crêpe into quarters and transfer to a warmed serving platter. Add the liqueur to the skillet and bring to a boil; boil about 30 seconds. Remove the skillet from the heat and add the butter, swirling the skillet until the butter is melted. Pour the hot sauce over the crêpes and serve at once.

½ **cup all-purpose flour**
4 **tablespoons sugar**
⅛ **teaspoon salt**
¾ **cup low-fat (1%) milk**
2 **large eggs, lightly beaten**
2 **teaspoons grated**
orange zest
⅓ **cup fresh orange juice**
2 **oranges, peeled and cut**
into segments (about
1½ cups)
2 **tablespoons orange-**
flavored liqueur, such as
Grand Marnier
3 **tablespoons light butter**

PER SERVING (1 crêpe with about ⅓ cup sauce): 178 Cal, 6 g Fat, 3 g Sat Fat, 0 g Trans Fat, 82 mg Chol, 84 mg Sod, 26 g Carb, 1 g Fib, 5 g Prot, 67 mg Calc. **POINTS** value: **4**

Sunshine Lemon Squares

❧

Hands-On Prep **20 MIN**
Cook **40 MIN**
Serves **16**

1 Preheat the oven to 350°F. Line an 8-inch-square baking pan with heavy-duty foil, extending it 2 inches beyond the sides (to create a "handle," so that the bars can easily be lifted out of the pan). Spray the bottom and sides of the foil with nonstick spray.

2 To make the crust, combine the ⅔ cup of flour, the vanilla wafer crumbs, the 2 tablespoons of granulated sugar, and the butter in a medium bowl, stirring until the mixture is the consistency of wet sand. Press the mixture into the bottom of the pan to form an even crust. Bake until firm, about 12 minutes.

3 Meanwhile, whisk together the 1 cup granulated sugar and the 2 tablespoons flour in a medium bowl. Whisk in the eggs, egg whites, lemon zest, and lemon juice until well blended, about 1 minute. Pour over the hot crust, return the pan to the oven, and bake until golden and set in the center, about 30 minutes. Cool completely in the pan on a rack. Lift out the whole square, holding on to the foil ends, and place on a cutting board. Remove the foil and cut into 16 squares. Sift confectioners' sugar on top (if using).

⅔ cup + 2 tablespoons
    all-purpose flour
⅓ cup vanilla wafer crumbs
2 tablespoons + 1 cup
    granulated sugar
3 tablespoons unsalted
    butter, melted
2 large eggs
2 egg whites
1 tablespoon grated
    lemon zest
½ cup fresh lemon juice
Confectioners' sugar
    (optional)

PER SERVING (1 square without confectioners' sugar): 119 Cal, 3 g Fat, 2 g Sat Fat, 0 g Trans Fat, 32 mg Chol, 2 mg Sod, 21 g Carb, 0 g Fib, 2 g Prot, 6 mg Calc. *POINTS* value: **3.**

Food Note You'll need about 4 lemons to get the ½ cup of fresh juice that this recipe calls for.

SUNSHINE LEMON SQUARES

Old-Fashioned Boston Cream Pie

❧

Hands-On Prep **25 MIN**
Cook **35 MIN**
Serves **12**

1 Custard: Whisk the granulated sugar, cornstarch, and salt in a medium saucepan. Whisk in the milk and egg. Cook over medium heat, stirring constantly, just until the mixture simmers. Cook, stirring constantly, until thickened, about 1 minute. Remove the pan from the heat; stir in the butter and vanilla. Press a piece of wax paper onto the surface; let cool.

2 Cake: Preheat the oven to 350°F. Spray two 9-inch nonstick round cake pans with nonstick spray. Sift the cake flour, baking powder, and salt; set aside. With an electric mixer on high speed, beat the eggs until thickened. Gradually add the granulated sugar, beating until fluffy. On low speed, add the water, butter, and vanilla, beating just until blended. Add the flour mixture, beating just until incorporated. Pour the batter into the pans. Bake 25–30 minutes; cool completely in the pans on racks. Unmold the cakes onto the racks.

3 Glaze: Sift the confectioners' sugar and cocoa into a small saucepan. Stir in the condensed milk and coffee. Heat over a low heat, stirring, until the mixture bubbles; cook 1 minute. Remove from the heat. Cool until thickened. Place 1 cake layer, bottom side up, on a plate. Whisk the custard and spread over the layer, leaving a ½-inch border along the edge. Top with the remaining layer, top side up. Spread the glaze on top.

PER SERVING (¹⁄₁₂th of cake): 224 Cal, 5 g Fat, 3 g Sat Fat, 0 g Trans Fat, 80 mg Chol, 212 mg Sod, 40 g Carb, 1 g Fib, 5 g Prot, 120 mg Calc.
POINTS value: **5.**

CUSTARD
⅓ **cup granulated sugar**
3 **tablespoons cornstarch**
¼ **teaspoon salt**
1½ **cups low-fat (1%) milk**
1 **large egg**
1 **tablespoon unsalted butter**
2 **teaspoons vanilla extract**

CAKE
1 **cup cake flour**
1½ **teaspoons baking powder**
¼ **teaspoon salt**
3 **large eggs, at room temperature**
¾ **cup granulated sugar**
¼ **cup hot water**
2 **tablespoons unsalted butter, melted**
1 **teaspoon vanilla extract**

GLAZE
⅓ **cup confectioners' sugar**
3 **tablespoons Dutch-process unsweetened cocoa powder**
½ **cup fat-free sweetened condensed milk**
½ **teaspoon instant-coffee powder**

Best Banana Cream Pie

Hands-On Prep **20 MIN**
Cook **15 MIN**
Serves **8**

1 To make the crust, preheat the oven to 375°F. Spray a 9-inch glass pie plate with nonstick spray. Put the graham crackers in a food processor or blender and pulse until finely ground. Add the honey, oil, and milk; process until crumbly. Press the mixture evenly into the bottom and up the sides of the pie plate. Bake until firm, about 9 minutes; cool completely on a rack.

2 To make the filling, whisk the sugar and cornstarch in a medium saucepan. Whisk in the milk, egg, and salt. Bring just to a simmer over medium heat, whisking constantly as the mixture begins to thicken. Let simmer, whisking constantly, about 30 seconds. Remove the pan from the heat; gradually whisk in the half-and-half and vanilla. Press a piece of wax paper onto the surface; let cool 15 minutes.

3 Slice 2 of the bananas in half lengthwise; cut crosswise into slices. Place the slices in an even layer on the bottom of the crust. Spread the filling evenly over the top. Press a piece of wax paper onto the filling and refrigerate until thoroughly chilled, at least 3 hours or overnight.

4 To serve, slice the remaining banana and toss with the lemon juice in a small bowl. Arrange on top of the pie and cut the pie into 8 wedges.

PER SERVING (1 wedge): 234 Cal, 5 g Fat, 1 g Sat Fat, 1 g Trans Fat, 29 mg Chol, 163 mg Sod, 46 g Carb, 1 g Fib, 4 g Prot, 80 mg Calc. *POINTS* value: *5.*

CRUST
- 9 (5 x 2½-inch) graham crackers
- 2 tablespoons honey
- 1 tablespoon canola oil
- 1 tablespoon low-fat (1%) milk

FILLING
- ½ cup sugar
- ¼ cup cornstarch
- 1½ cups low-fat (1%) milk
- 1 large egg
- ⅛ teaspoon salt
- ½ cup fat-free half-and-half
- 1 teaspoon vanilla extract
- 3 medium ripe bananas
- ½ tablespoon fresh lemon juice

CHERRY-ALMOND
CRISSCROSS PIE;
BERRY-NECTARINE
COBBLER, PAGE 195

Cherry-Almond Crisscross Pie

Hands-On Prep **25 MIN**
Cook **1 HR**
Serves **10**

1 Crust: Pulse the flour, confectioners' sugar, and salt in a food processor until blended. Add the shortening and butter; pulse until the mixture is crumbly. Combine the water and vinegar; add to the flour mixture and pulse just until combined. Shape the dough into 2 disks, one slightly larger than the other. Wrap and refrigerate until chilled, about 1 hour.

2 Preheat the oven to 425°F. Between floured sheets of wax paper, roll out the larger disk to form a 13-inch circle. Fit into a 9-inch pie plate. Leaving a 1-inch border, trim off any excess dough; add the trimmings to the remaining dough. Between floured sheets of wax paper, roll out the dough to form a 9½ x 7-inch oval. Cut lengthwise into ½-inch strips.

3 Filling: Combine the ½ cup cherry juice, brown sugar, lemon juice, and almond extract in a bowl. Whisk in the cornstarch until smooth; then add the cherries. Spoon the filling into the crust.

4 Weave the strips of dough in a lattice pattern on top of the filling. Crimp the edges of the crust; cover with strips of foil to prevent overbrowning. Bake 30 minutes. Reduce the heat to 350°F. Bake until the crust is golden and the filling is bubbly, 30–40 minutes. Cool on a rack at least 3 hours.

PER SERVING (¹⁄₁₀th of pie): 218 Cal, 7 g Fat, 2 g Sat Fat, 1 g Trans Fat, 6 mg Chol, 180 mg Sod, 38 g Carb, 2 g Fib, 2 g Prot, 22 mg Calc. *POINTS* value: **5.**

CRUST
- 1½ **cups all-purpose flour**
- 1 **tablespoon confectioners' sugar**
- ¾ **teaspoon salt**
- 3 **tablespoons vegetable shortening**
- 2 **tablespoons unsalted butter, cut into small pieces**
- 4½ **tablespoons cold water**
- ¾ **teaspoon white vinegar**

FILLING
- 2 **(15-ounce) cans pitted dark cherries, packed in juice or light syrup, drained (reserving ½ cup juice)**
- ½ **cup packed light brown sugar**
- 1 **tablespoon fresh lemon juice**
- ¼ **teaspoon almond extract**
- 3 **tablespoons cornstarch**

Florida Key Lime Pie

Hands-On Prep **15 MIN**
Cook **10 MIN**
Serves **10**

1 To make the filling, pour the lime juice into a small bowl and sprinkle with the gelatin. Let stand until the gelatin is softened, about 5 minutes. Transfer to a small saucepan and heat over low heat, stirring occasionally, until the gelatin dissolves, about 2 minutes.

2 Stir in the condensed milk and cook, stirring occasionally, until heated through, about 5 minutes. Remove the pan from the heat and let cool 10 minutes. Transfer to a large bowl and refrigerate until the filling starts to set, about 30 minutes.

3 Whisk the thickened filling until creamy and smooth; stir in the lime zest. With a rubber spatula, gently fold in the whipped topping, stirring until combined. Pour the filling into the pie crust and refrigerate until firm, at least 3 hours or overnight. Just before serving, garnish with the lime slices.

½ cup fresh lime juice
2 teaspoons unflavored gelatin
1 (14-ounce) can sweetened condensed milk
2 teaspoons grated lime zest
1½ cups thawed fat-free whipped topping
1 (9-inch) reduced-fat graham cracker crust
1 small lime, thinly sliced

PER SERVING (⅒th of pie): 240 Cal, 7 g Fat, 5 g Sat Fat, 1 g Trans Fat, 18 mg Chol, 130 mg Sod, 40 g Carb, 0 g Fib, 4 g Prot, 119 mg Calc. *POINTS* value: *5.*

Try It Look for genuine key limes from Florida in better supermarkets. They are smaller, with golden-yellow flesh, and slightly more tart than the ubiquitous Persian lime. If they're not available, use Persian limes. Just don't use bottled lime juice; it has an unwelcome, slightly tinny flavor. You'll need 3 to 4 Persian limes or 10 to 12 key limes for this recipe.

Southern Sweet-Potato Pie

❧

Hands-On Prep **25 MIN**
Cook **40 MIN**
Serves **8**

1 Crust: Pulse the flour, confectioners' sugar, and salt in a food processor until blended. Add the shortening and butter; pulse until crumbly. Combine the water and vinegar in a cup; pour through the feed tube, pulsing just until the mixture is combined. Flatten the dough into a disk; wrap and refrigerate until chilled, at least 1 hour.

2 Preheat the oven to 375°F. Between floured sheets of wax paper, roll out the dough to form a 13-inch circle. Fit the circle into a 9-inch pie plate, crimp the edges, and prick the bottom with a fork. Line the crust with foil, folding the foil over to cover the edge. Bake 12 minutes. Remove the foil; pierce any bubbles in the crust with the tip of a knife. Bake until lightly browned, about 8 minutes. Let cool.

3 Reduce the heat to 350°F. Bring to a boil in a medium saucepan the potatoes and enough cold water to cover. Reduce the heat and simmer until fork-tender, about 45 minutes. Drain and cool. Mash in a large bowl until smooth. Measure 1⅓ cups puree (reserving any extra for another use) and return it to the bowl. Whisk in the eggs, egg whites, and brown sugar until smooth. Whisk in the remaining ingredients until blended. Pour the filling into the crust. Bake until the center is just set, 35–40 minutes. Cool completely on a rack.

PER SERVING (⅛th of pie): 267 Cal, 6 g Fat, 2 g Sat Fat, 0 g Trans Fat, 58 mg Chol, 368 mg Sod, 46 g Carb, 3 g Fib, 7 g Prot, 111 mg Calc. **POINTS** value: **5.**

CRUST
- 1 cup all-purpose flour
- 1 tablespoon confectioners' sugar
- 1 teaspoon salt
- 2 tablespoons vegetable shortening
- 1 tablespoon unsalted butter, cut into 6 pieces
- 3 tablespoons cold water
- ½ teaspoon white vinegar

FILLING
- 2 large sweet potatoes (1½ pounds), peeled
- 2 large eggs
- 3 egg whites
- ½ cup packed dark brown sugar
- ¾ cup evaporated fat-free milk
- 1 tablespoon fresh lime juice
- 1 teaspoon pumpkin-pie spice
- ½ teaspoon salt
- ¼ teaspoon freshly ground pepper

Spectacular Baked Alaska

Hands-On Prep **20 MIN**
Cook **3 MIN**
Serves **10**

1 Spray a 9-inch pie plate with nonstick spray. Line the bottom of the plate with slices of cake, cutting pieces as needed to fill any holes. Cut the remaining slices in half lengthwise and place them around the edge of the plate, patching any remaining gaps. Freeze until firm, at least 20 minutes.

2 Remove the pie plate from the freezer and immediately spread the ice cream over the cake. Freeze 20 minutes; remove from the freezer and spread the sorbet evenly over the ice cream. Freeze until solid, 2–4 hours.

3 Place an oven rack on the center rung of the oven. Preheat the oven to 450°F.

4 With an electric mixer on low speed, beat the egg whites and cream of tartar in a medium bowl until soft peaks form, about 4 minutes. Increase the speed to high and gradually add the sugar, beating until stiff and glossy, about 3 minutes longer.

5 Remove the pie plate from the freezer and mound the meringue over it, spreading to the edge of the plate to cover the sorbet completely. Bake until the meringue is just golden brown on top, 3–4 minutes. Serve at once.

6 (½-inch) slices fat-free pound cake (about 10 ounces)
1 pint vanilla reduced-fat ice cream, softened
1 pint raspberry sorbet, softened
6 large egg whites, at room temperature
⅛ teaspoon cream of tartar
¾ cup sugar

PER SERVING (¹⁄₁₀th of pie): 240 Cal, 1 g Fat, 0 g Sat Fat, 0 g Trans Fat, 1 mg Chol, 165 mg Sod, 54 g Carb, 0 g Fib, 5 g Prot, 58 mg Calc.
POINTS value: **5.**

Italian Tiramisu

❧

Hands-On Prep **25 MIN**
Cook **NONE**
Serves **12**

1 Combine the boiling water, espresso powder, and the 1 tablespoon of sugar in a medium heatproof bowl; stir until the espresso powder and sugar are dissolved and let cool slightly.

2 Spray a 9 x 13-inch glass baking dish with nonstick spray. Line the bottom with the cake slices, cutting some pieces as needed to fill any gaps. Brush with the espresso mixture to saturate the cake; set aside.

3 Put the cream cheese, the additional 1 cup sugar, and the vanilla in a food processor and process just until smooth; transfer to a large bowl. Gently fold in the whipped topping and spread over the cake. Top evenly with the chocolate. Cover with plastic wrap, being careful not to let the wrap touch the surface of the tiramisu, and refrigerate until chilled, at least 4 hours or up to 3 days.

½ cup boiling water
5 teaspoons instant-espresso powder
1 tablespoon + 1 cup sugar
1 (13-ounce) fat-free pound cake, cut into ½-inch slices
2 (8-ounce) packages tub-style fat-free cream cheese
1 teaspoon vanilla extract
1 (8-ounce) tub frozen fat-free whipped topping, thawed
4 ounces semisweet chocolate, finely chopped

PER SERVING (about 3 x 2-inch piece): 268 Cal, 4 g Fat, 2 g Sat Fat, 0 g Trans Fat, 6 mg Chol, 345 mg Sod, 50 g Carb, 1 g Fib, 8 g Prot, 191 mg Calc. ***POINTS*** value: **5.**

Plan Ahead One of the great things about this dessert is that it can be made up to 3 days in advance—and it only gets better as the flavors develop.

Warm Chocolate-Pudding Cake

❧

Hands-On Prep **15 MIN**
Cook **35 MIN**
Serves **9**

1 Preheat the oven to 350°F. Spray a 9-inch-square baking pan with nonstick spray.

2 Combine the flour, granulated sugar, the ⅓ cup of cocoa powder, the baking powder, espresso powder, baking soda, and salt in a large bowl. Make a well in the center, and pour in the milk, melted butter, and vanilla. Stir just until blended; spoon the batter evenly into the pan.

3 Combine the brown sugar and the additional ¼ cup cocoa powder in a small bowl. Sprinkle evenly over the batter. Gently pour the boiling water in a zigzag fashion over the top; do not stir. Bake until the top of the pudding is set, about 35 minutes. Cool on a rack at least 30 minutes. Cut into 9 squares and serve warm or at room temperature.

¾ **cup all-purpose flour**
¾ **cup granulated sugar**
⅓ **cup + ¼ cup unsweetened cocoa powder**
2 **teaspoons baking powder**
1 **teaspoon instant-coffee powder**
¼ **teaspoon baking soda**
¼ **teaspoon salt**
½ **cup low-fat (1%) milk**
1 **tablespoon unsalted butter, melted**
1½ **teaspoons vanilla extract**
⅓ **cup packed dark brown sugar**
1⅔ **cups boiling water**

PER SERVING (1 square): 165 Cal, 2 g Fat, 1 g Sat Fat, 0 g Trans Fat, 4 mg Chol, 220 mg Sod, 37 g Carb, 2 g Fib, 3 g Prot, 94 mg Calc.
POINTS value: **3.**

Good Idea Serve this fudgy favorite with a scoop of vanilla or coffee fat-free frozen yogurt; ½ cup with each serving will increase the **POINTS** value by **2**.

WARM CHOCOLATE-PUDDING CAKE

Ultra-Chocolate Malt

Hands-On Prep **5 MIN**
Cook **NONE**
Serves **3**

Pour the milk and ice cream into a blender and puree. Add the syrup and malt powder; puree until smooth and frothy. Serve at once.

1½ cups fat-free milk
1 cup chocolate reduced-fat ice cream
2 tablespoons light chocolate syrup
2 tablespoons malt powder

PER SERVING (1 cup): 168 Cal, 4 g Fat, 2 g Sat Fat, 0 g Trans Fat, 13 mg Chol, 123 mg Sod, 29 g Carb, 0 g Fib, 7 g Prot, 227 mg Calc. *POINTS* value: **4.**

Good Idea For an even bigger dose of chocolate in every sip, use chocolate-flavored malt powder; the per-serving **POINTS** value will remain the same.

Creamy Orange Shake

❧

Hands-On Prep **5 MIN**
Cook **NONE**
Serves **4**

Put the ice cubes in a blender and pulse until crushed. Add the sherbet, yogurt, milk, and juice concentrate; puree until smooth.

PER SERVING (1 cup): 135 Cal, 1 g Fat, 1 g Sat Fat, 0 g Trans Fat, 4 mg Chol, 71 mg Sod, 28 g Carb, 0 g Fib, 4 g Prot, 144 mg Calc.
POINTS value: *3.*

Food Note If you like, substitue orange sorbet for the sherbet for an extra citrusy blast of flavor.

1 cup ice cubes
1 cup orange sherbet
1 cup sugar-free vanilla fat-free frozen yogurt
1 cup fat-free milk
2 tablespoons thawed frozen orange juice concentrate

SUNSHINE LEMON SQUARES, PAGE 204

Dry and Liquid Measurement Equivalents

If you are converting the recipes in this book to metric measurements, use the following chart as a guide.

TEASPOONS	TABLESPOONS	CUPS	FLUID OUNCES
3 teaspoons	1 tablespoon		½ fluid ounce
6 teaspoons	2 tablespoons	⅛ cup	1 fluid ounce
8 teaspoons	2 tablespoons plus 2 teaspoons	⅙ cup	
12 teaspoons	4 tablespoons	¼ cup	2 fluid ounces
15 teaspoons	5 tablespoons	⅓ cup minus 1 teaspoon	
16 teaspoons	5 tablespoons plus 1 teaspoon	⅓ cup	
18 teaspoons	6 tablespoons	¼ cup plus 2 tablespoons	3 fluid ounces
24 teaspoons	8 tablespoons	½ cup	4 fluid ounces
30 teaspoons	10 tablespoons	½ cup plus 2 tablespoons	5 fluid ounces
32 teaspoons	10 tablespoons plus 2 teaspoons	⅔ cup	
36 teaspoons	12 tablespoons	¾ cup	6 fluid ounces
42 teaspoons	14 tablespoons	1 cup minus 2 tablespoons	7 fluid ounces
45 teaspoons	15 tablespoons	1 cup minus 1 tablespoon	
48 teaspoons	16 tablespoons	1 cup	8 fluid ounces

VOLUME	
¼ teaspoon	1 milliliter
½ teaspoon	2 milliliters
1 teaspoon	5 milliliters
1 tablespoon	15 milliliters
2 tablespoons	30 milliliters
3 tablespoons	45 milliliters
¼ cup	60 milliliters
⅓ cup	80 milliliters
½ cup	120 milliliters
⅔ cup	160 milliliters
¾ cup	175 milliliters
1 cup	240 milliliters
1 quart	950 milliliters

LENGTH	
1 inch	25 millimeters
1 inch	2.5 centimeters

OVEN TEMPERATURE			
250°F	120°C	400°F	200°C
275°F	140°C	425°F	220°C
300°F	150°C	450°F	230°C
325°F	160°C	475°F	250°C
350°F	180°C	500°F	260°C
375°F	190°C	525°F	270°C

WEIGHT	
1 ounce	30 grams
¼ pound	120 grams
½ pound	240 grams
1 pound	480 grams

NOTE: Measurement of less than ⅛ teaspoon is considered a dash or a pinch. Metric volume measurements are approximate.

Recipe Index

POINTS value Recipe Index

Fusilli with Creamy Gorgonzola Sauce, 108

Grilled Lamb Chops with Artichoke Relish, 127

Herbed Bubble Bread with Sun-Dried Tomatoes, 183

Meatball and Barley Soup, 75

Mesclun with Roasted Beets and Cheese Croutons, 62

Mini-Meatloaves, 123

Nachos Deluxe, 14

Oatmeal with Fresh Berry Sauce, 49

Orange-Cranberry Scones, 50

Orange-Glazed Quick Bread, 189

Orecchiette with Broccoli Rabe, 114

Panna Gotta with Berry Sauce, 202

Pizza-Style Cauliflower Bake, 169

Snapper with Herbed Bread Crumbs, 154

Southern Zucchini-Corn Bread, 185

Sun-Dried Tomato and Sausage Focaccia, 11

Tex-Mex Meatloaf, 125

Turkey and Black Bean Chili, 131

Twice-Baked Potatoes with Feta Cheese, 161

Ultra-Chocolate Malt, 216

5 POINTS value

Apple-Cheddar Pancakes, 40

Bacon-and-Egg Muffin Melt, 28

Baked Chicken Parmesan, 144

Berry-Nectarine Cobbler, 195

Best Banana Cream Pie, 207

Cheesy Tortilla Casserole, 155

Cherry-Almond Crisscross Pie, 209

Crunchy Chicken Bake, 145

Florida Key Lime Pie, 210

Green Goddess Cobb Salad, 55

Ham-and-Cheese Spoon Bread, 38

Hearty Shepherd's Pie, 139

Hearty Split-Pea Soup, 76

Hearty Stuffed Cabbage, 126

Herb-Stuffed Pork Chops, 140

Home-Style Lentil Soup, 87

Italian Tiramisu, 213

Italian-Bread Soup, 78

Macaroni and Cheese, 152

New England Fish Chowder, 82

Old-Fashioned Boston Cream Pie, 206

Pasta with Red Clam Sauce, 104

Pasta with Tomatoes, Goat Cheese, and Basil, 109

Penne with Vodka and Tomato, 110

Pork Tenderloin with Summer Fruit, 128

Southern Sweet-Potato Pie, 211

Spectacular Baked Alaska, 212

Speedy Pizza Margherita, 116

Triple-Cranberry Baked Apples, 193

Turkey Tetrazzini Bake, 149

6 POINTS value

Capellini with Seafood and Herbs, 102

French Onion Soup, 90

Italian Salad Pizza, 118

Mama's Baked Ziti with Meatballs, 100

Mediterranean Chicken Casserole, 148

Pasta Salad with Pesto and Tomatoes, 64

Peanut-Butter French Toast, 45

Pear Dutch Baby, 42

Rigatoni Bolognese, 99

Rigatoni with Spinach, Ricotta, and Raisins, 111

Soufflé Omelette with Fruit Compote, 35

Spaghetti alla Carbonara, 101

Thai Noodles with Tofu, 107

Tuna-Noodle Casserole, 151

7 POINTS value

Banana-Oat Pancakes, 39

Baked-Bean and Pork Casserole, 142

Buttermilk Corn Cakes, 41

Date and Almond Oatmeal, 47

Easy Vegetable Lasagna, 105

Ginger Salmon en Papillote, 150

Ham and Bell Pepper Calzones, 112

Louisiana Gumbo, 79

Seared Scallops with Fresh Corn Relish, 133

8 POINTS value

Southwest Pizza, 115

Veggie and Cheddar Pizza, 117

Notes